LEGACY

LEGACY

PORTRAITS OF 50 BAY AREA ENVIRONMENTAL ELDERS

Photographs by

Nancy Kittle

Text by

John Hart

SIERRA CLUB BOOKS

San Francisco

The Sierra Club, founded in 1892 by John Muir, has devoted itself to the study and protection of the earth's scenic and ecological resources— mountains, wetlands, woodlands, wild shores and rivers, deserts and plains. The publishing program of the Sierra Club offers books to the public as a nonprofit educational service in the hope that they may enlarge the public's understanding of the Club's basic concerns. The point of view expressed in each book, however, does not necessarily represent that of the Club. The Sierra Club has some sixty chapters throughout the United States. For information about how you may participate in its programs to preserve wilderness and the quality of life, please address inquiries to Sierra Club, 85 Second Street, San Francisco, California 94105, or visit our website at www.sierraclub.org.

The author wishes to thank Brendan Furey of the Regional Oral History Office of the University of California, Berkeley, Talya Gould and Andrew Olsen of the San Francisco Foundation, and Mark Sarfati for assistance in locating the photograph on p. 32.

Book and jacket design by Elizabeth Watson

Published by Sierra Club Books
85 Second Street, San Francisco, CA 94105
www.sierraclub.org/books

Produced and distributed by
University of California Press
Berkeley and Los Angeles, California
University of California Press, Ltd.
London, England
www.ucpress.edu

SIERRA CLUB, SIERRA CLUB BOOKS, and the Sierra Club design logos are registered trademarks of the Sierra Club.

Library of Congress Cataloging-in-Publication Data
Kittle, Nancy, 1930-
     Legacy : portraits of 50 Bay Area environmental elders / photographs by Nancy Kittle ; text by John Hart.— 1st ed.
        p. cm.
     ISBN 1-57805-151-7 (alk. paper)
     1. Environmentalists—California—San Francisco Bay Area— Biography. 2. Conservationists—California—San Francisco Bay Area— Biography. I. Hart, John, 1948-   II. Title.

     GE55.K58 2005
     333.72'092'279461—dc22
     [B]   2005045056

Printed in Italy
First Edition
09 08 07 06
10 9 8 7 6 5 4 3 2 1

Photo on page 2: Sylvia McLaughlin at Eastshore State Park, 1997

To my impatient mentors at art school,

John Collier, Jr., and Jerry Burchard

—N.K.

CONTENTS

PHOTOGRAPHER'S PREFACE

—◊—

In the late 1990s, when I was casting about for a new photo project, a friend suggested senior environmentalists. Since I am a fully qualified senior (with a memory of Pearl Harbor) and a long-time supporter of environmental causes, the idea seemed a good fit. The few potential subjects to whom I spoke were warmly enthusiastic, and soon I had a growing list of candidates.

With the exception of the archival photo of Esther Gulick, Kay Kerr, and Sylvia McLaughlin, I have taken all of the book's images myself—whenever possible, at sites having particular significance for the individuals. In one case, this required considerable rock scrambling, but typically, we simply needed to make a number of attempts.

It is important to keep in mind the date of each portrait. Those who were photographed at the start of the project had the advantage of relative "youth" in contrast to the more recent participants. No matter what age these elders were when the shutter clicked, however, they all accepted the challenge of posing for the camera with good humor and grace.

Unfortunately, delays in the project have meant that some of the subjects are no longer here to see the book that honors them. To their families and friends I offer my sincere apologies together with my hopes that the book will please and touch them. Finally, to these heroes and heroines, I give my heartfelt thanks for your patience and, above all, for being who you are and for what you have done.

—Nancy Kittle

Defenders of Place

—⚬—

It seems at times as though some green-plumed guardian angel were hovering over the San Francisco Bay Area, protecting its environment from harm.

Granted, as population in the nine counties touching the Bay has risen to 6.7 million, the usual penalties of growth have been incurred. Farm and woodland have given way to cities; pollution constantly challenges our efforts to control it; a sprawling style of development, which consumes much land to house relatively few people, has become the unfortunate norm. Many natural values have been irrevocably lost. Yet what strikes visitors from other burgeoning regions is not our failure but our success—how well we've done here at hanging on to some of the best features of the place we live in.

We have always in view—even when we don't take time to enjoy—the shimmering expanses of San Francisco Bay, not filled in and built on as once was extensively planned. North from San Francisco we have the Golden Gate National Recreation Area and Point Reyes National Seashore, composing a vast, accessible greenbelt that hardly another American metropolis can match. We have a comparable greenbelt under construction in the south, in the Santa Cruz Mountains and along the San Mateo coast. We have the superlative East Bay Regional Parks. We have numerous state and federal wildlife refuges, and a roster of native plants and animals that, despite enormous pressures, has suffered relatively few outright deletions.

And we have all these things, not in most cases because a benevolent government provided for them, but because certain stubborn individual citizens felt called upon to work for them, often against great odds.

The legacy comes down to us from a generation of environmental leaders born in the 1930s or earlier. These are people who remember, and in many cases fought in, World War II. Most of them made their commitment to the conservation cause well before the first celebration of Earth Day in 1970, which is sometimes regarded as a sort of environmental Big Bang, the origin of everything green. Some had been active for decades by that year and already had great achievements under their belts.

This book portrays and honors some fifty of these extraordinary people. Nancy Kittle originated the project and made the photographs. The text is based on interviews conducted by Christina Russo, China Galland, and myself, supplemented by oral histories in the Bancroft Library at the University of California, Berkeley. Though accessible facts have been checked, this is essentially a book of personal memories and should be read as such.

We claim no comprehensiveness. Some great names are missing. Dorothy Erskine, open space champion and founder of what became the Greenbelt Alliance, should be here. So should the scholar Mel Scott, a key contributor to the preservation of San Francisco Bay, and Peter Behr, the North Bay state senator who helped to block dams on California's wild northern rivers. Caroline Livermore, godmother of conservation in Marin County, appears often but indirectly in these pages. These and other champions of the Bay Area environment died before this project was conceived.

Inevitably, there have been additional losses between conception and publication. David Brower is gone. Raymond Dasmann. Esther Gulick. Kay Holbrook. Doris Leonard. Margaret Owings. Will Siri. Ledyard Stebbins. Dwight Steele. Bill and Ellen Straus. Peggy Wayburn. We have chosen to show our cast in a sort of eternal present, active as they were when we met them.

These environmental elders take their places in an even longer story. In the late nineteenth and early twentieth centuries, there were already two issues that conservation-minded Bay Area citizens rallied around: city parks and redwoods.

San Jose, one of the oldest towns in the region, was the very first to set aside a tract of land for public recreation. In 1866, it created Alum Rock Park around an area of hot springs in the foothills east of town. Now just one of many parks in those hills, the spot was once a famous weekend destination, promoted as "Little Yosemite."

In the same era, the landscape architect Frederick Law Olmsted, designer of New York's Central Park, spent some time in San Francisco and lamented that the only public open space in the booming city was a hilltop cemetery. He proposed a great park west of Twin Peaks. In 1870, the city laid out Golden Gate Park in the uninhabited dunes toward the Pacific shore. The object here was not to preserve a landscape but to transform one; the austere natural scene gave way to a friendlier swathe of trees, lawns, lakes, buildings, and roads. The thousand-acre playground was for decades the largest recreation area in the Bay Area.

Oakland, the third early population center of the region, dreamed of a comparable achievement. In 1907 the city acquired for public use the immediate shoreline of Lake Merritt, the tidal basin near the historic core of town, one of the community's great assets today.

Meanwhile local citizens were watching in distress as the last of the region's coast redwoods fell to the saws. In 1900, Andrew Putnam Hill, a San Jose painter and photographer, founded a group called the Sempervirens Club (still in existence as the Sempervirens Fund) with the goal of preserving the magnificent old-growth trees along Waddell Creek north of Santa Cruz. After various rebuffs, Hill laid siege to the legislature, organizing what may have been the state's first environmental letter-writing campaign. In 1902, a wearied Governor Henry Gage signed a bill creating the 3,800-acre California Redwood Park, the first preserve of its kind. Greatly expanded since, it is known as Big Basin Redwoods State Park today.

In Marin County, too, the story begins with redwoods. On the south side of Mount Tamalpais, one inaccessible stand had reached the twentieth century unlogged. In 1905, a local civic leader and tree lover named William Kent stepped in to buy the site. Then a water company filed suit to take the property for a reservoir. Going right to the top, Kent persuaded President Theodore Roosevelt to accept donation of the land for a federal park—to be named, at Kent's insistence, Muir Woods National Monument, in honor of John Muir, the already famous conservationist and founder of the Sierra Club.

Kent actually wanted the whole of Mount Tamalpais reserved for the public. He applauded when the Marin Municipal Water District, founded in 1912, bought the north slopes of the mountain as a watershed for its reservoirs, keeping the land open for quiet recreation.

In 1917, fifty miles farther north, the County of Sonoma protected an additional sequoia forest near the Russian River, now Armstrong Redwoods State Park.

At the end of World War I, these six areas—Alum Rock, Golden Gate, Lake Merritt, Big Basin, the Mount Tamalpais complex, and Armstrong Redwoods—made up the region's entire stock of large public parks.

Between the world wars the pace of preservation increased. In 1927, the legislature passed three bills important to the region. One brought the state park system into being. A second, enacted in response to a threatened subdivision, established Mount Tamalpais State Park adjacent to Muir Woods National Monument. A third allowed for the creation of local park districts by public vote.

In 1928, the East Bay Municipal Utilities District purchased the lands of a private water company in Alameda and Contra Costa Counties and proposed to sell off extensive areas not needed for water supply but valuable for recreation. Civic leaders hurriedly organized an East Bay Regional Park District to buy these scenic lands. By 1940, Tilden Regional Park, Redwood Regional Park, and several other parks on the ridge above Berkeley and Oakland were on the map. Even more important for the future was the existence of the park district itself, endorsed by the voters, funded by taxes, and in the market for more land. It would go on to acquire properties the founders had never dreamed of, from islands in San Francisco Bay to historic mines north of Mount Diablo.

After World War II the growth of the Bay Area cities began in earnest. Suburbs spread in all directions; old downtowns became mere nodes in a mass of urban tissue. Landfills pushed out into San Francisco Bay. Freeways multiplied, and transit systems struggled to keep up. Air and water pollution emerged

as metropolitan problems. And conservation efforts, too, took on a whole new scale.

In the 1950s, for the first time, we see citizens petitioning city councils and boards of supervisors to turn down development proposals outright. We see activists pushing for more restrictive zoning as well as for bigger parks. And we see a convergence between the goals of conservationists and the ideas of urban planners. Local controversies are increasingly seen in the context of a larger question: What should the emerging regional metropolis look like, and in what manner should it grow?

The fourteen years from 1958 to 1972 transformed the region's approach to its lands and waters. In this period, the Bay and the coastline were saved from landfill and rampant development; new, sweeping greenbelts were created; pollution was confronted; and new government bodies with environmental mandates came into being one after another. This decade and a half stands out as a kind of heroic era in Bay Area conservation. Among its major actors were the people in this book.

The "firsts" unfold year by year.

In 1958, a group of planners and conservationists met in San Francisco to launch a group called Citizens for Regional Recreation and Parks. Its purpose was larger than its name, for what it really wanted was a regional blueprint for conservation and development; its head, Dorothy Erskine, had begun her career as an expert on housing.

In the same year, a federal survey found the Point Reyes Peninsula in Marin County to be one of the most valuable stretches of undeveloped coastline left in the United States. Agitation began for a national park on this pastoral shore.

In 1961, the region's attention turned to the condition of San Francisco Bay. The Army Corps of Engineers published a map showing that most of the Bay was shallow enough to be filled, if current trends continued. Citizens for Regional Recreation and Parks called a conference on the Bay, and three East Bay women, alarmed at Berkeley's ambitious bay fill plans, launched the enormously effective Save San Francisco Bay Association (Save the Bay).

In that same year the region's counties and cities got together to form the Association of Bay Area Governments (ABAG), a regional planning forum. ABAG began work on a land use plan for the entire nine-county region, addressing the all-important question of what areas should become urban and what areas should not.

In 1962, Congress brought Point Reyes National Seashore into existence. Even today, Point Reyes is perhaps the finest of the region's open spaces. Near the other end of the Bay Area, the Committee for Green Foothills was founded in Palo Alto to oppose urban development in the Santa Cruz Mountains.

In 1965, responding to tremendous public pressure, the state legislature established the San Francisco Bay Conservation and Development Commission. It was at first a temporary body, charged with controlling bay fill while it prepared a plan for management of the Bay and its shores.

It was also in 1965 that the "San Francisco Freeway Revolt" came to its climax. After years of controversy, the city's board of supervisors turned down an offer some thought could not be refused: the state's plan to build freeways through Golden Gate Park and along the northern waterfront. Opponents of the many other freeways proposed for sensitive areas throughout the region took heart.

In the same year, a group of citizens in San Mateo and Santa Clara Counties began pushing for a San Francisco Bay National Wildlife Refuge to include remnant tidal marshes and bird-friendly salt evaporation ponds around the southern reaches of the Bay.

In 1966, the Marin County Board of Supervisors approved a massive development in the Marin Headlands near the Golden Gate. Marincello seemed unstoppable, but a handful of local lawyers, offended by the way the plan had been rammed through, set out on an ultimately successful campaign to derail it in court.

In 1967, the California Air Resources Board was created, signaling the first serious effort to do something about smog.

In 1968, the board of supervisors of Napa County decided that the famous Napa Valley vineyards were more valuable than the urban development that threatened to engulf them. They decreed that agricultural properties could not be split into parcels smaller than twenty acres. It was the first such ordinance to be passed in the United States.

In 1969, the Bay Conservation and Development Commission published its *San Francisco Bay Plan,* calling for an end to bay fill. By the narrowest of margins, the legislature made the commission and its policies permanent.

In the same year, the state took aim at water pollution with the Porter-Cologne Act. The sewage and industrial discharges that were fouling San Francisco Bay came under the control of the San Francisco Bay Regional Water Quality Control Board.

In 1970, the Association of Bay Area Governments published its *Regional Plan 1970–1990.* To the surprise of many—though not of the conservationist insiders who had influenced the process—it called for the curbing of suburban sprawl. Future growth, the plan proclaimed, should be compact, centered on existing cities, and contained in a framework of open space. About one-fifth of the land in the nine Bay Area counties should be urban; the rest should be greenbelt, forever or at least for the very long term.

In Sacramento, the lawmakers passed the California Environmental Quality Act, which requires that the environmental effects of proposed developments be openly assessed before decisions are made. The legislature also created a Metropolitan Transportation Commission to oversee Bay Area transportation planning.

In 1971, the San Francisco–based planning and environmental organization California Tomorrow brought forward a draft of its *California Tomorrow Plan:* a model of how environmental and social problems might be met by a revamped system of state government. Among other proposals, the plan envisioned regional governments, with elected legislatures, covering every part of the state.

Meanwhile, a move was afoot to create a national park around the Golden Gate, including the Presidio and other obsolescent U. S. Army bases on both shores and extending north into Marin County through the site of Marincello and beyond.

Nineteen seventy-two was a year of harvest:

- Congress enacted the Golden Gate National Recreation Area in its maximum form, reaching all the way to the gates of Point Reyes National Seashore and linking preexisting parks to form a greenbelt of 120,000 acres. At the same moment, Marin County adopted new plans for the rural western reaches of the county. Where once it had foreseen a horizon of suburbs, it now committed itself to maintaining West Marin as open landscape for ranching and for recreation.
- The campaign for the San Francisco Bay National Wildlife Refuge also ended in success. The 23,000-acre refuge was the first such ever designated in an urban zone in the United States.
- The Midpeninsula Regional Open Space District was set up to buy open space in the Santa Cruz Mountains.
- President Nixon signed the federal Clean Water Act, guaranteeing federal money for local efforts at pollution control.
- In an amazing climax, state voters alarmed at coastal development and loss of access created a California Coastal Zone Conservation Commission, modeled on the Bay Commission, to manage growth along a thousand miles of ocean shore.

What might 1973 do to top all that? As the year started, change was still in the air. The legislature seemed ready to pass a law to stop the paving over of the state's best agricultural lands. And it was seriously debating the obvious next step for the San Francisco Bay Area: creation of a limited regional government, absorbing several recently established single-purpose agencies, and led by a partially elected regional council or board. Only such a body, it was felt, could really grapple with the region's problems and guide its future.

It took a while for advocates to realize that nothing much more was going to happen, at least for the time being.

After so many years of innovation, exhaustion seemed to have set in. Rival reform proposals were canceling each other out. Existing government bodies were digging in to defend their powers. And the door to structural change, flung wide for a moment, was swinging back to its normal position, open at best a crack. It shut with an almost audible click in 1978, when the voters of the state enacted Proposition 13, a constitutional provision that sharply cut property taxes and, more significantly, required a two-thirds popular vote to raise taxes of any kind whatsoever.

Why this pendulum swing occurred is a matter for historians, sociologists, and perhaps psychologists to debate. For environmental activists, it was simply a new condition to adjust to, a change of political weather.

Their task for the remainder of the twentieth century was largely to build on the foundations laid through 1972: to support the Bay Commission and the Coastal Commission in their work, to complete and expand the bold new parks and refuges, to ride herd on pollution control agencies. Where those foundations had been left incomplete, the challenge was to accomplish by local and often by private means what regional and statewide government bodies could not.

One of those half-built foundations was the open space scheme delineated by the Association of Bay Area Governments in its 1970 plan. Though this vision had been universally applauded, it was only a vision. Local governments might or might not take the plan into account as they confronted specific development proposals; in most cases, they did not.

Conservationists stepped into the breach in two ways: by backing local efforts to buy strategic open spaces and by urging cities and counties to adopt growth patterns similar to those in the ABAG plan.

On the land acquisition side, dramatic progress has been made, especially in San Mateo and Santa Clara Counties. Without much fanfare, an arc of publicly owned lands is taking shape along the Coast Range highlands from Sweeney Ridge near San Francisco to Big Basin Redwoods State Park. Key properties continue to be purchased in other Bay Area counties as well. Many of the new parks and open spaces serve to contain development by blocking the corridors along which new suburbs might extend.

On the political front, more and more Bay Area local governments have in fact adopted plans that conform to the 1970 open space vision. To make sure that these decisions stick, the Greenbelt Alliance (successor to Citizens for Regional Recreation and Parks)

has pushed a legal device called the "urban growth boundary": a stated outer limit for development, often locked in by the electorate. Some twenty jurisdictions in Alameda, Marin, Santa Clara, and Sonoma Counties have imposed such boundaries on themselves.

Opposing development where it shouldn't be is only half a strategy. The other half is to support development where common sense says it should be: near transit stations, for example; in underused and rundown areas that need investment; and on small parcels skipped over in the first wave of growth. This "infill" development, which raises density somewhat, also raises some hackles; but most of the region's conservation leaders now see it as the way to go.

In the 1990s, a new great project got underway in the Bay Area, one that recalls the high hopes of 1970: the ecological restoration of San Francisco Bay.

Though bay fill has been halted and pollution reduced, the Bay, known to scientists as the San Francisco Estuary, is still a greatly impaired natural system. One key to restoring its health, the experts say, is to let the Bay grow again by breaking some of the dikes that long ago dried out its margins. Where development has not pressed too close to the water—in the South Bay, along the north rim of San Pablo Bay, and in Suisun Bay east of the Carquinez Strait—the opportunity exists to restore huge tracts of tidal marsh, with tremendous benefits to wildlife and people. Pilot projects have already begun in many places. What is proposed is a work of ecological restoration of planetary significance.

Plainly, there is everything to be done—and any amount of room for heroes yet to be.

Bay Area environmental activism has provided a model for the world, and not only because some local activists stepped into wider roles. The successful fight to block freeways through Golden Gate Park and along the San Francisco waterfront was a shot heard across the nation. The Save the Bay effort produced the first regulatory body of its kind on the planet. Napa and Marin Counties were pioneers in farmland preservation. The list goes on and on.

As the journalist Harold Gilliam points out, Bay Area leaders have a habit of taking on seemingly hopeless campaigns—and winning: "Other places heard about what happened here and began to realize that victory was possible after all, in spite of the fact that the biggest interests were on the other side, the big money was on the other side. People power got it done." Or as Sue Bierman, a leader in the 1960s Freeway Revolt in San Francisco, puts it: "People just rise up and care."

What motivates that caring?

Most of our subjects can name two specific places that formed their green sensibility. The first is a landscape encountered in youth that gave them an inner picture of how things should be. For David Brower, for example, the model was the Berkeley Hills when they were nearly wild. For Lois Crozier-Hogle, it was Huntington Lake in the central Sierra Nevada. For Harold Gilliam, it was a waterfall in the Hollywood Hills. One spot on the California landscape is mentioned most often, as a first or supplemental trigger: Yosemite Valley. To later comers the valley suffers somewhat from its iconic status—and its perennial crowding. It seems a bit of a mess and a bit of a cliché. Not to the people in this book. Seeing it for the first time in the 1920s or 1940s, they often found tears in their eyes.

The second key imprint, typically, is the place that draws a person across the difficult threshold between attitude and action—between saying "Somebody ought to do something" and saying "Here I come." Sometimes the battleground is a place known from childhood, sometimes not. For Amy Meyer, that spot was East Fort Miley, a sort of vacant military lot in San Francisco. For Dwight Steele, it was Lake Tahoe. For Lennie Roberts, it was a stand of old-growth redwoods on the Navarro River. For Ledyard Stebbins, it was an arboretum in Berkeley.

Our heroes are a diverse lot. They have worked on various levels, by various means. Some are activists, some are educators, some are funders. Some, like Robert Praetzel, stepped forward to tackle a single local issue, then moved back to the fringes of the fray; others, once launched, had lifetime conservation careers. Some, like Kay Holbrook, are forever associated with one place; others addressed the region, the state, or the world. Still others have broadened their focus on a different axis to include social problems other than the environmental. Near the wide end of this spectrum are Martin Rosen and Huey Johnson; alone at the extreme of it is Alfred Heller, stubborn advocate of a statewide planning system that would give all needs their due.

Standing a little to one side is a subgroup of scientists, planners, and writers, technical people in their differing ways, mostly eschewing group affiliation and influencing events indirectly, by shifting the state of knowledge and the climate of opinion. Ledyard Stebbins and Luna Leopold, for instance, have approached the world as researchers; Harold Gilliam and Raymond Dasmann have spoken to it through the power of the pen.

Many of our subjects know each other. There are relationships of affection, collaboration, mentoring, but in some cases of irritation, even enmity. The environmentalist family is as conflict-prone as any other. For instance, anyone who belonged to the Sierra Club in the 1960s remembers the internal fight that cost David Brower his job as executive director. The episode is forever raw to those involved, a kind of environmental Dreyfus Affair.

That confrontation also reflected a perennial split between leaders who might be called Warriors and those who might be called Negotiators. The Warriors are permanent rebels, impatient with half-measures, putting environmental needs ahead of all others, wary of alliances of convenience. David Brower is the model. The Negotiators have a calmer passion and are adept at the inside game. Ike Livermore, who served in the cabinet of California Governor Ronald Reagan and gave that administration a respectable environmental record, comes to mind. Some people on either side of this divide see the other approach as ineffective. Yet each kind of energy demonstrably has had its hour.

In its formal politics, the group is bipartisan, or multipartisan, covering the range from moderate Republican to Green. In an age of polarization, this variety is refreshing. Some leaders have translated their concern into modest political careers, either at the beginning of their work, like Eleanor Boushey, or toward the end, like Jean Siri. Most have not.

Half of the cast of characters are women, and most of these spent years managing households and raising children. Far from feeling restricted by this "house-wife" role, they took advantage of it to create volunteer careers that made significant marks on the world. Who could possibly be patronizing to an Amy Meyer, a Sylvia McLaughlin? Try it and see.

Many of these environmental pioneers have money. Not a few might be said to belong to an elite. They have had leisure for their environmental work; they have also, in some cases, had valuable connections. These advantages they have used for the greater good.

Given the time when they emerged onto the scene, the relentless whiteness of this cast of characters is not surprising. More troubling is the fact that today's environmentalist community has about the same pale hue. A number of our witnesses worry about this, and several—David Brower, Jean Siri, Martin Rosen—have made energetic efforts to bring in people of other than European ethnic backgrounds, as well as reaching out to interest groups like unions.

One thing these veterans indubitably have in common is experience. They've been around. What advice might they have for young people starting out in the field? Some declined to offer any. "I wouldn't have the nerve," Kay Holbrook said. Martin Litton remarked that *he* as a young man wouldn't have accepted, or welcomed, any such advice. But some were more forthcoming, and even the reticent teach by example.

Six practical lessons do appear to emerge.

Lesson #1: *Begin by beginning.* Over and over again the message comes: don't jump into the big picture, just find something specific that stirs your interest and start paying attention to it. Find out what's going on, who the players are, what decisions are coming up. If other people are working on the matter, meet them. Simply take hold.

Lesson #2: *Go to the damned meeting.* Especially at the local level, our system of government gives uncommon weight to those who simply show up. Elizabeth Terwilliger made a practice of hanging out at local government meetings whether or not an issue of concern to her was on the table. More and more, she says, "they listened to me."

Lesson #3: *Do your homework.* Good advocates learn their subject in depth. Lennie Roberts urges, "Get so knowledgeable about what you are talking about that nobody can ask you a question that you cannot answer."

Lesson #4. *Keep on keeping on.* As much as anything else, success for these leaders has been a matter of sheer doggedness. The occasional march to triumph, such as the campaign for the Golden Gate National Recreation Area in the early 1970s, is the exception. Trench warfare is the norm. These successful activists never stopped showing up. They absorbed many setbacks. They chipped away. They were always there. And very often they prevailed. One of Ike Livermore's colleagues in Governor Reagan's cabinet groused, "The sun never sets on a Livermore argument." You could substitute many another name.

The other two guidelines are mentioned less often but frequently enough to note.

Lesson #5: *Be scrupulous in argument.* For many if not all of these environmental leaders, it has been a rule to distinguish fact from opinion and to avoid overly selective presentation of the data. The reward—reported surprisingly often—is the trust of people in power. Lois Crozier-Hogle tells how San Mateo County planning officials came to rely on information from her Committee for Green Foothills, saying: "We can depend on it, it's accurate." Dwight Steele reports winning this respect even from outright opponents. "That takes a long time to develop," he adds.

Lesson #6: *Don't burn bridges—build them.* Many of our people caution against making permanent enemies in the heat of battle. Sylvia McLaughlin refers to her "honorable opponents." Martin Rosen says, "My approach always seeks to make allies out of adversaries."

The following gallery of portraits is arranged in an order that is partly chronological, partly geographical, partly thematic, and now and then associational, pursuing links among friends.

The series begins with a few noble unclassifiables. Then we meet a group of people known above all for their work on San Francisco Bay, followed by landscape savers from the coastal counties, Santa Clara, San Mateo, San Francisco, Marin, and Sonoma.

Next we turn to people who have affected the scene by methods less direct but by no means less profound: writers, scientists, educators, and a few of the deep-pocketed folk whose generosity fuels the hopes and labors of the rest.

A final group—to which many an earlier profile could be shifted—comprises leaders whose stories plainly transcend the region: whose mark has been made on a statewide, national, and even planetary scale.

Sue Bierman

—m—

One day in 2001 a limousine pulled up in front of Sue Bierman's home near the Golden Gate Park Panhandle in San Francisco. In it was Mayor Willie Brown. Instead of the meeting she thought she was going to, Bierman found herself whisked a short block down to the park and into a ceremony to unveil a plaque in someone's honor: hers.

On a sunny morning two years later, she sits in the same spot among the boles of noble trees from several continents, hearing the shouts from a playground her children once used. She tells the story of the freeway that would have destroyed this precious urban amenity and how, to the astonishment of a national audience, the plan was stopped.

Bierman arrived in the Bay Area from Michigan in 1953 with her philosophy professor husband, Arthur Bierman. She had rather hoped that his academic career would take them to New York, but when she found herself in San Francisco, the bond was quick to form. "I'm happy we came, now. Thrilled!"

Within sight of the Biermans' new home was a wooded knoll known as the Montgomery Property. It belonged to the city, which however planned to sell it off. Bierman and her neighbors protested to the Park and Recreation Commission. "I don't know why she's so upset," Bierman recalls a commissioner saying. "Nothing but a bunch of raccoons up there. Just a bunch of raccoons." But the small green parcel is part of the city's Interior Park Belt today.

That was a rehearsal.

In the 1950s, California's freeway network was exploding. Californians think they have quite a few freeways now; the dreamed-of network would have been several times as large. Construction seemed to be going on everywhere at once. People who objected, because they were displaced or because open spaces or neighborhoods were going under, were considered cranks. The state had decided that only one mode of transportation really mattered, the private automobile. At all costs, its path must be eased.

In 1952, the city and the state agreed on a plan for nine different freeways crisscrossing San Francisco; the sketch looked like a tic-tac-toe grid. "San Francisco Skyways to Ease Traffic, Open Up Vistas," the *Chronicle* headlined in 1954. But neighborhood resistance started early, and in 1959 the board of supervisors cut the proposed network to the two routes regarded as essential. The Golden Gate Freeway, curving along the northern waterfront, would link the Bay Bridge to the Golden Gate Bridge; the Embarcadero Freeway (demolished in

Sue Bierman seated on a bench dedicated to her in the Golden Gate Park Panhandle in San Francisco, 2003

1990) was its bud. The second, also feeding the Golden Gate, would carve its way through central San Francisco, displacing hundreds of mostly black families in the Western Addition before reaching another zone of supposedly low resistance, Golden Gate Park. While the main body of the park would have suffered only a gash, the narrow eastern extension known as the Panhandle, one block wide and eight blocks long, would simply have been destroyed.

This phase of the controversy lasted seven more years. It polarized San Francisco, straining old alliances and bringing new ones into being. Two daily newspapers became cheerleaders—the *Examiner* in favor of the freeways, the *Chronicle* now against. As the closeness of the battle became apparent, the national media arrived, smelling one of those "only in California" stories. In the thick of it all was Sue Bierman.

The key, the activists recognized, was to keep the neighborhoods united in opposing both freeways at once. Some people felt tempted to accept one plan as the price of stopping the other, and the Division of Highways deftly hinted at compromise. "But people really stuck together," Bierman says. "We all just *knew*. Because they would talk with us. 'Well, if we don't do *this*, maybe we could get support?' No. No support."

In 1966, as the final vote approached, the board of supervisors seemed to be leaning against the freeways—by a one-vote margin. "It was just touch and go," Bierman recalls. "We'd have it all set, and then we'd hear that one was flaking." Reportedly one undecided supervisor spent the final weekend in the bathtub, trying to calm his nerves and make up his mind. Sue Bierman herself broke out in nosebleeds. Then, on March 21, the decision fell. Against both freeways:

Supervisors William Blake, Roger Boas, Terry Francois, Eugene McCarthy, and George Moscone. For both freeways: supervisors Joseph Casey, Kevin O'Shea, Peter Tamaras, and Joseph Tinney. For the Golden Gate but not the Panhandle: Jack Morrison. For the Panhandle but not the Golden Gate: John Ertola. Thus each route was defeated, 6 to 5.

"There will be a freeway on the moon before we get one in San Francisco," Mayor John F. Shelley lamented. But the city has survived, neither worse nor better off in traffic terms, it seems, than towns that bowed to the logic of the highway engineers.

Looking back, the 1966 vote seems an important tipping point. Certainly the Bay Area would be a very different place today if the California Division of Highways had carried out more of its plans. The best efforts of local conservationists would have withered in the face of freeways into West Marin, freeways down the San Mateo County coast, and the several additional bridges that were proposed over the years.

The San Francisco Freeway Revolt, as the journalist Harold Gilliam dubbed it, also reverberated statewide, nationally, even around the world. It did not mark the end of a transportation policy organized around the private automobile. But it signaled that there could at least be real debate about such things, real battles, in which the conventional engineering wisdom would not always prevail.

"I would never be a pessimist," says Sue Bierman, who went on to many roles in San Francisco politics. "I really like to work with people. And this city, no matter when, always has had, if you can find them, the people who care. We sure found them with this fight. People just rise up and care."

Ike Livermore

—⁓—

Norman B. Livermore, known to the world as Ike, became a hero to conservationists as resources secretary to Governor Ronald Reagan from 1966 to 1974. It happened somewhat to the surprise of all concerned.

During his state cabinet service, Livermore stopped an ecosystem-busting dam on the Eel River, blocked a long-planned highway across the middle of the great Sierra Nevada wilderness, midwifed the creation of Redwood National Park, and supported conservation efforts in countless quiet ways. Because of Livermore, Reagan's record as governor is more than a little "green."

Livermore's earlier life seems to have groomed him for that season of opportunity. He is one of five sons of Caroline Livermore, an early leading light of conservation in Marin County. But from his father, Norman senior, an engineer and businessman, he learned a keen respect for nuts-and-bolts economics and a certain skepticism about do-gooder schemes. "I saw both sides," says Livermore. "I'm a meld between the two."

Livermore grew up in San Francisco and Marin and attended the outdoorsy Thacher School in Ojai. At age fifteen, in 1929, he rode horseback two hundred fifty miles north from Ojai to Monterey, following the rugged Big Sur coastline. At the time, Highway One had not yet been pushed through the region, and Livermore wishes it never had been. He would later tease his friends Margaret and Nathaniel Owings, Big Sur residents: "If you're really pure and sincere wilder-

ness people, you'd vote for blasting that road out. Get rid of it, because it ruined that fabulous coast."

In that same summer, on a camping trip to Mendocino County, he got acquainted with some national forest rangers. Their dedication and way of life appealed to him. He felt he had found a calling.

But when Livermore graduated from high school in 1929, Forest Service jobs were scarce. After knocking on many government doors, he went to work instead for a private packer, an outfitter taking parties of riders and hikers into the Sierra wilderness. This was the trade he plied almost every summer for twenty years, first as an underling and later as proprietor of one of the largest pack operations in the Sierra. "There are fifty passes in the High Sierra higher than ten thousand feet. I have been over every single one of those, in both directions.

"The first real trip I went on, we went the whole length of the John Muir Trail. We hit a certain spot near the Minarets. We'd had a long, tough day. This packer kept talking about this beautiful meadow that we were going into. And when we got there, there were automobiles in it. It was just like a stab to my heart."

That spot was on the banks of the uppermost San Joaquin River, west of the town of Mammoth Lakes. The Sierra crest is low in this section, and even in the 1920s a road from Mammoth dipped over the crest and started down the Pacific slope before ending at Livermore's campsite. It seemed inevitable that that highway would someday be pushed on through to meet a similar route coming up from the west side. Conservationists dug in their heels to keep the wilderness unbroken, and for forty years the matter remained unresolved.

In the 1930s and 1940s, Livermore was active in the Sierra Club, which was also one of his chief clients for trips. It was a letter from him that started the ball rolling toward the first of several Sierra Club Wilderness Conferences, and arguably toward passage of the Wilderness Act of 1964, the great charter of American roadless area preservation. But by 1949 Livermore was pulling back, finding in the Club a visceral hostility to business that made him uncomfortable.

In 1952 he took a job with Pacific Lumber, where he worked as treasurer for fifteen years. He watched with dismay the growing controversy over redwood logging and urged the industry to moderate its practices, for instance by leaving uncut strips along highways.

In 1966, out of the blue, came the call from Governor-elect Ronald Reagan's staff asking him to take on the California Resources Agency post.

The big environmental debate in California in those years concerned the proposed Redwood National Park. Livermore was by no means convinced that there should be a federal park; but if there was to be one, he wanted it to be a respectable area. Gradually he won a skeptical Governor Reagan around to his point of view. The park that was created in 1968, though an awkward compromise, would have been far smaller without his support.

Then there was the Minarets Road, the long-proposed route that would have bisected the Sierra roadless area and interrupted the John Muir Trail. In 1972, Livermore took a keen and personal pleasure in leading the administration to kill this road, and later saw the controversy end when Congress made the corridor part of the newly established Ansel Adams Wilderness.

Another hot potato of the time was the proposed Dos Rios Dam, which would have tapped the Eel River system for the State Water Project, turned remote Round Valley in northern Mendocino County into a huge reservoir, and opened the way for exploitation of all of California's North Coast rivers. Uninformed at the outset about California water policy, Livermore learned on the job. He concluded that the benefits of the project did not justify the cost in dollars and in damage to fish and other natural resources—and the drowning of an Indian reservation. Livermore went so far as to signal to the governor that he would resign if the plan was approved. To the consternation of the agencies and interest groups that made up the "water establishment," Reagan nixed the project. A few years later, the Eel and the other great rivers of the North Coast were placed in the federal Wild and Scenic Rivers System, the aquatic parallel to Wilderness status.

Since his days steering state resource policy, Livermore has filled many conservation roles behind the scenes. In particular, he has never missed a chance to work on the problems of his beloved Sierra Nevada.

A tantalizing moment came in 1980, when he traveled to Washington, D.C., as a key member of the transition team for the incoming president, his old California boss. Might Livermore be Ronald Reagan's secretary of the interior? "Had I been offered the job," he says, "I think I would have been hard put to refuse it."

But other counsel prevailed, and the nation's top conservation post went instead to a man whose views could hardly have been more at odds with Livermore's: the notorious James Watt.

Ike Livermore at his family's ranch, Montesol, in Napa County, 1998

Margaret Owings

—ɯɯ—

One wild winter morning in 1973, Margaret Wentworth Owings stood at the great window of her home on the Big Sur Coast and looked out, as she often does, for sea otters. The day before she had watched a pair of the animals clinging to strands of kelp that whipped back and forth in the waves. Now they were gone. "They have simply worn out, bashed against the rocks," she thought. "A defeat."

But at noon she picked up the binoculars again, surveying a calmer world. "There, below our house, a relaxed little otter lay on his back on the sea, his hind feet out flat, his tail stretched out like a blade of grass. Not a hundred feet away another otter lay, rocking like a cradle. On her chest, her forepaws embraced the dandelion-white fluff of a newborn pup.

"For a moment," Owings goes on, "the meaning of what I witnessed was more than I could handle."

Margaret Owings—artist, friend of Rockefellers and Roosevelts, Ansel Adams, Robinson Jeffers, Georgia O'Keefe—belongs to what might be called the animal rights wing of environmentalism. She has always identified with living things as individuals and striven to protect them.

Owings grew up in the part of Berkeley known as Thousand Oaks in the 1920s, when the neighborhood still deserved the name. In a field across the road grew Johnny jump-ups, baby blue eyes, brodiaeas. "Neighborhood children would come around and pick them and I'd shout, 'Oh no! Don't pick them. Leave them there!'"

In school at Mills College, she had a rug made of a mountain lion skin, complete with bullet hole. "I felt badly about that bullet hole. It was evidence of the cougars being hunted, and that distressed me."

In 1937, she moved to Chicago with her first husband, but never stopped feeling essentially Californian, often returning on vacation. She recalls one visit to the Monterey coast after an oil spill. "We went to the Point Lobos sea gardens, and they were lined with black tar and oil. I looked and I thought, 'This is it. This is the end. This is the way it's going to be.'"

The switch from fatalism to action came a little later, after divorce, relocation, and remarriage. By 1953 she was living on a wild stretch of the Big Sur coast in a house she had built with her second husband, the architect Nathaniel Owings. Wildlife was all around her, creatures so present that she became aware of them as personalities. Hunters were everywhere, too. When the Steller sea lion bull she liked to watch was shot, she wrote protest letters to the *Monterey Peninsula*

Margaret Owings at Wild Bird, her home in Big Sur, 1997

Herald and became known as the "sea lion lady." Then she learned of a bill, sponsored by the fishing industry, to "cull," or kill, three quarters of the sea lions in the state. "That night, after I read about the sea lions, I cried. Nat said, 'Now let's not cry about it any more, and tomorrow morning we'll begin to work.'" In the next few days the couple pulled together a Committee to Save the Sea Lions, studded with such famous names as the naturalist A. Starker Leopold, the photographer Ansel Adams, the National Park Service pioneer Horace Albright, and the philanthropist Laurence Rockefeller. The culling bill died in three weeks.

"That's the way I nearly always start on anything," Owings says. "I do it because a bomb has gone off right under my nose and I can't walk away from it. People click their tongues and shake their heads and keep right on going, but I can't. I have to leap right into it."

The next bomb went off in 1962, when a female cougar that roamed the Owings property was shot. The greater upset was to read in the paper that the mountain lion hunter had been rewarded with state money for disposing of a "bountied predator." Again Owings tapped her enormous network and her own eloquence to create a Committee to Repeal the State Bounty on the California Mountain Lion and, later, the Mountain Lion Foundation. The bounty was abolished in 1963, but the larger campaign to halt lion hunting continued until 1990, when the California voters formally declared the cougar a "protected species."

Then, and perhaps most famously, there was the sea otter. As with the sea lion, conflict arose because the animals ate the same prey valued by human harvesters—in this case, by abalone divers. To see an otter munching on an abalone made them furious. They demanded control. One evening in 1968, after attending a contentious meeting on the issue, Owings realized that she was on the hook again. "We walked over to that north window, because we always made our decisions at that north window. We stood there, and I said, 'I'm going to have to form Friends of the Sea Otter, Nat.' I sat down at our dining table and designed a mother and pup. Anything I start, I have to draw it first. Here it is. That is my stationery."

Over the years, Friends of the Sea Otter has won several victories for the species. It secured protection for the otter under the Endangered Species Act. It got gill nets banned from shallow water, which saved many otters from death by entanglement and drowning. Scientific study increased. But the population is still stagnant, for reasons unclear, and human shellfish harvesters still regard the otter as a troublesome competitor for the crop.

When she feels despondent about setbacks, Margaret Owings takes strength from her view of the ocean horizon. "Living here, and walking out on the porch, and looking at the immensity of the world . . . man's troubled ways and greedy ways, all those things that bother me so much, they fall apart. I look at the big planet that's left there, I see this big turn of the planet, and it makes me feel that way."

30

Esther Gulick, Kay Kerr, and Sylvia McLaughlin

—◊—

There was a place called San Francisco Bay before there was a place called San Francisco. California's first city took its name from the body of water, not the other way around. And the larger metropolis that has since enveloped the great harbor is known simply as the San Francisco Bay Area. It is one of the few urban regions to take its identity from a natural feature.

In the century after the Gold Rush, though, the region honored its treasure in name only. By 1960, San Francisco Bay was facing severe degradation. It was badly polluted by industry, agriculture, and domestic sewage. Its shoreline was largely locked away in industrial and military uses. And the Bay was physically shrinking as its shallower waters began to be filled with garbage and rubble to create new buildable real estate.

Not a few people around the water's edge saw what was happening and shook their heads. In Marin County, the conservationist Caroline Livermore organized an effort to save 900 acres of tidelands in Richardson Bay from impending fill. In Palo Alto, a waterfront development was blocked. But it was in Berkeley that three extraordinary women launched the unprecedented effort that truly "saved the Bay."

The three were rooted in the University of California culture. Esther Gulick's husband, Charles, taught eco-

nomics on the Berkeley campus. Sylvia McLaughlin's husband, Don, served on the Board of Regents of the multi-campus University of California system. And Kay Kerr's spouse, Clark, was the system's president.

The three women had something else in common: hillside houses with windows facing San Francisco Bay. From the McLaughlin and Gulick homes in Berkeley and from the Kerr home in El Cerrito, the water was an inescapable, delightful presence.

All were aware, as the 1950s passed, of encroachments on the waterscape below. Gulick, who frequently traversed the Bay Bridge on family business, may have been the first to take alarm. "Crossing the Bay and seeing what was happening to it, and also smelling it when you go down the shoreline, made me realize that something that I had loved and had grown up thinking was always going to be here . . . maybe wasn't going to be."

Kay Kerr recalls a morning in her living room in 1960. "Esther Gulick was here for a cup of tea, and we were looking across the Bay, and on the left there was smoke coming up because the garbage dump at Albany was being burned, and there was a bulldozer down here at Point Isabel pushing dirt into the Bay, where there had been a beautiful little cove. We agreed that it was too bad you had to look so far away to see how

31

pretty everything was, because it wasn't very nice to look close."

A little later, at the Town & Gown Club near the campus, Kerr heard of a bigger threat. "Sylvia McLaughlin was talking with me, and she said, 'Do you know, it's terrible what Berkeley's planning to do; they're planning to double the size of the city by filling in the Bay. I think it's awful.' And I said, 'I do too.' And the lady next to her said, 'Well, you need to have three people, and then you can change the world.' I said to Sylvia, 'I know who the third person is. Do you want to come up for a cup of tea?'"

And so the famous Bay-saving triumvirate, or triumfeminate—Gulick, Kerr, and McLaughlin—convened for the first time.

The three didn't know how conservation battles worked; they had no intention of founding an organization. At first they merely hoped to focus attention on the problem—and to pass it on to more experienced hands.

In January 1961, they made their case to a roomful of conservation leaders invited to the Gulick home. In Kay Kerr's account: "I remember Dave Brower saying, 'Well, it's just exceedingly important, but the Sierra Club is principally interested in wilderness and in trails.' The next guy, Newton Drury, said, 'This is very important, but we're saving the redwoods, and we can't save the Bay.' It went around the room to the point where there was dead silence. So we said, 'Well, the Bay is going to go down the drain.' Dave Brower said, 'There's only one thing to do: Start a new organization, and we'll give you all of our mailing lists.' They all wished us a great deal of luck, and they went out the door."

So began the Save San Francisco Bay Association, usually just known as Save the Bay. Harold Gilliam, in attendance at the seminal meeting, didn't think much of its chances. But in two years it was a major force in the region. In a decade it had achieved its goal.

In retrospect it is clear that these women had access to two very different, and complementary, kinds of power. One was high-level and came, fundamentally, through their husbands. They were socially in contact with politicians, academic experts, and business leaders. The second type of power came from below. Concern about the Bay, though still subterranean, was running deep in the region. The thought that there was hope—a chance—something really to be done—brought it bubbling out, like artesian water, with a wholly unexpected force.

Gulick, Kerr, and McLaughlin split the chores. Gulick ran the office, keeping track (on handwritten file cards) of thousands upon thousands of one-dollar memberships. Kerr was the writer, producing a series of pithy, influential flyers on particular issues and threatened stretches of shoreline. McLaughlin was the public speaker, telling the story to audiences far and wide.

The women found themselves students again. They had to speak with authority about everything from migratory birds to tides to airports to planning law. McLaughlin recalls cramming, in the car on the way to a Sacramento hearing, for an anticipated question on anadromous fish. "We needed to learn about these things very quickly," she says, "so we did."

"It kind of bothered me," McLaughlin confesses. "Here we were, three housewives, telling professional people what they should be doing." She mentioned her reticence to her university friend Jack Kent, a professor (and important advocate) of regional planning. "And

From left: Sylvia McLaughlin, Esther Gulick, and Kay Kerr about to receive the
Robert C. Kirkwood Award from the San Francisco Foundation in San Francisco, 1985

he looked at me, and in a very definite way, said, 'Sylvia, you can do whatever you determine you want to do.' So after that, I didn't worry so much."

A key moment came when Eugene Lee, director of the university's Institute of Governmental Studies, found $5,000 to produce a report called *The Future of San Francisco Bay*, researched and written by the eloquent planning scholar Mel Scott. It was Scott who proposed the idea of a special agency to limit shoreline fill, to be called perhaps the San Francisco Bay Conservation and Development Commission.

So the idea was there. Persuading the state legislature to turn it into reality was quite another matter. Here Save the Bay found an ally in Gene McAteer, an ambitious and effective state senator from San Francisco—and a Kerr family friend. Aware of the powerful interests to be confronted, McAteer devised a kind of creeping strategy. In 1964, he got the legislature to authorize a brief pilot study. In 1965, a second law created the Bay commission as a temporary agency, with power to halt fills while it wrote a plan for use of the Bay and shoreline. Finally, in 1969, the legislators made

the Bay Conservation and Development Commission a permanent state agency.

If it seems like a march to inevitable victory, that was far from the feeling at the time. There was formidable opposition from would-be developers. The final vote was a cliffhanger: the Bay was saved, in the end, by a one-vote margin in the state senate.

After 1969, Save the Bay had more hard work ahead, fending off attacks on the young commission and making sure it did its job. Life took the Kerrs away from the Bay Area for a number of years. Esther Gulick and Sylvia McLaughlin remained active in Bay affairs, and McLaughlin went on to work on larger scales, national and international.

McLaughlin is also a leader in the coalition called Citizens for East Shore Parks, which works to increase public access and conserve habitat along the waterfronts of Berkeley and adjacent cities. In 2002, an extensive Eastshore State Park came into being. The hillside windows through which three remarkable women once saw the degradation of San Francisco Bay now frame a vista of public, protected shores.

Joe Bodovitz and Mel Lane

In the fall of 1965, the new state commission to control the filling of San Francisco Bay opened its doors. But establishing the Bay Conservation and Development Commission was one thing. Making it work was quite another. Many interests looked for it to fail. That BCDC functioned and survived is often credited to two quiet insiders named Joe Bodovitz and Mel Lane. They have been colleagues, friends, and one another's best character references for more than forty years.

Lane, a native Californian, was part of the family team that managed *Sunset*, the successful "lifestyle" magazine headquartered in Menlo Park. Oklahoma-born Bodovitz was a relative newcomer; he had gotten to know the region as a port of call during the Korean War and returned to start what he thought would be a journalistic career with the *San Francisco Examiner*.

"Like everybody in journalism," Bodovitz says, "I thought I was going to be a foreign correspondent." Instead, he had found himself on the local government beat, covering the school board, the planning commission, the redevelopment agency—the droning rooms where the undramatic decisions are made that actually shape cities and lives. To his surprise, he got hooked. He saw how the system worked when it worked well, when it worked badly, when it didn't work at all. He formed a lifelong devotion to good process—not as opposed to good results, but in the faith that the one would lead to the other.

This mindset led him in 1962 to a job at one of those private organizations that were bridging planning and environmental concerns, the San Francisco Planning and Urban Renewal Association.

In those days the effort to stop bay fill was just getting under way. The first tentative step toward control was a pilot study, mandated by the state legislature, lasting a mere four months. The study group needed a staff, but Bodovitz notes that "there were not a lot of people eager to quit their jobs for a four-month thing." His boss, John Hirten, gave him the right kind of short-term leave.

"The study commission was in some ways the most fun I ever had," Bodovitz says. "Those are the kind of things you do because you don't know you can't do them. We held twelve public hearings, all over the Bay Area, and we commissioned a couple of consultant studies, and by working our tails off we put out a really jazzy book and report."

That work led to the establishment, in 1965, of the first, temporary San Francisco Bay Conservation and Development Commission (BCDC). Bodovitz—the closest thing to a veteran the new field afforded—was the obvious choice to head the staff. At this point he met Mel Lane, whom Governor Pat Brown had appointed as chair of the commission. Friends in the Brown circle had backed Lane as the ideal leader: a Republican businessman, well known through *Sunset*,

not alarming to the interests with whom he would be dealing, and deeply concerned for the public good.

Lane and Bodovitz, wary at first, soon recognized in each other a similar spirit, a kind of passionate scrupulousness.

BCDC had the awkward task of deciding on shoreline development proposals in the present while writing, for the future, the very plan needed to guide those decisions. "People came to us to be approved or not approved on the basis of our saying, 'This will or will not be in conflict with legislation that we haven't yet written,'" Lane says. He chuckles. "They had a good complaint, but we didn't see any other way to do it."

"None of it would have happened without Mel Lane as chairman," Bodovitz says. "His ability to make everybody feel good about the hearings and give everybody a fair shake . . . just made it all possible."

Making the Bay Plan, Lane recalls, was a learning process for all concerned. Commissioners who started with very different outlooks tended to converge in their thinking over time. "When you look at the total of something, by and large people agree." Most decisions were unanimous.

One of the toughest lessons concerned the nature of property rights on the muddy bottom of the Bay. Much of the bay floor was, on paper, privately owned, the result of sweeping grants made by the state in the nineteenth century. But under an ancient doctrine called the "public trust," the water overlying such land remains public property, to be kept open to such uses as fishing and boating. You can own your piece of the bay bottom, all right, but you have no resulting right to fill it in.

"People who owned those mudflats," Lane says, "thought they had a great opportunity to dump a lot of dirt on them, to create a new shoreline, and get some free real estate. And it was a real educational job to show them that they couldn't do it."

In 1969, the commission published its plan and gained its status as a permanent agency. Protection of the open waters of the Bay has been a given since then, part of the de facto regional environmental constitution.

The success of the BCDC opened the way for a much bigger experiment. Frightened at a rash of new developments along the 1,100-mile ocean coast of California, conservationists went to the legislature to seek a similar body to manage coastal growth and protect shoreline access. Blocked in Sacramento, the advocates put their plan on the ballot. In 1972, after a fierce campaign, the voters established the California Coastal Zone Conservation Commission—six regional coastal commissions, actually, and an overarching statewide one.

Again the team of Bodovitz and Lane was tapped to get things going at the top, with Lane as commission chairman and Bodovitz as executive director. Bodovitz went nervously, aware that the coastal planning show was opening before a partly hostile audience. "If we just floundered and looked like a bunch of people who couldn't figure out what to do, clearly the whole notion would be discredited. Somehow or other when the doors opened we had to be on top of things." Thanks to the two men, and to staff support provided by California Resources Secretary Ike Livermore, a smooth start was achieved.

Like BCDC before them, the state and regional Coastal Commissions were temporary. They had to write a plan, make the case for their own continuation, and meanwhile handle day-to-day decisions up and

Joe Bodovitz at home in Mill Valley, 2005

down the coastal strip. The commissioners found themselves weighing the most varied aspects of urban and rural life. "Forestry. Nude beaches in the south. Everything except snow removal," Bodovitz marvels. "Everything under the sun."

One of the things under the sun was the San Onofre nuclear power plant near San Diego, an issue both men recall as a test. Two utilities had spent years seeking permission to build this power station on the Camp Pendleton Marine Corps Base. Under the new coastal law, they had to ask again. Finding some issues worth a second look—the leveling of scenic bluffs, the effect on the nearby ocean of hot water discharge—the commission turned down the plant as proposed. "You can imagine the headline in the *Los Angeles Times*," Lane says. But the goal was to improve the plan, not kill it, and the plant was built—at a much-lowered environmental cost.

"I was in a funny position," Lane muses, "publishing a magazine selling advertising. A lot of the people who were behind those big projects were my customers. They certainly leaned on me at times."

In 1976, a restructured California Coastal Commission, shorn of its regional subcommissions, was made a permanent state agency. A few years later, Lane and Bodovitz moved on. Bodovitz served a stint as executive director of the California Public Utilities Commission. Lane helped to launch the Peninsula Open Space Trust; he has been a trustee of The Sierra Club Foundation and a director of the World Wildlife Fund.

Lane has also served on the board of the National Trust for Historic Preservation, which makes grants to protect and restore old buildings and neighborhoods. This, too, he counts as an environmental pursuit. By putting vitality back into historic downtowns, the Trust helps fight the decentralizing tendencies of sprawl.

In 1985 Mel Lane and Joe Bodovitz joined forces again in a new nonprofit venture, the California Environmental Trust. Here they bring their eighty years of combined experience to bear in mediating environmental disputes in their trademark way: without much noise, without much flash, with respect for all points of view, and very much behind the scenes.

Mel Lane in his garden in Atherton, 2000

Jean and Will Siri

—∿—

When climber, nuclear physicist, and conservationist Will Siri set off for Nepal in 1954 to lead an expedition up the great Himalayan mountain Makalu, he lived with his wife, Jean, in a hillside home in Richmond. When he returned six months later, it was to an address in El Cerrito. Nothing had moved but a boundary. Dissatisfied with Richmond city services, Jean found a way for their hillside street to change jurisdictions. It was also during that half year that she really got going on her own career as an environmental activist.

Jean Brandenburg came to the Bay Area from North Dakota to study medicine, a pursuit she dropped in order to free up money for the education of two brothers. She went to work instead running the animal research section at Donner Laboratory in Berkeley, part of the University of California. There she met Will Siri, who had come to the region to take part in the atomic bomb project. Both later moved up the hill to the Lawrence Berkeley National Laboratory, where Will did pioneering work on the medical uses of nuclear radiation, writing the first book on the subject. "That's the book I typed," Jean remembers. "Oh, how boring!"

After their marriage in 1949, the two took up climbing. "He always wanted to, and so he dragged me into it, kicking and screaming," Jean remembers.

"Wherever there's a rock outcrop in the Bay Area, I think we've climbed it." They went on to more ambitious trips in the Sierra and elsewhere, and Will to some of the most arduous peaks in the world.

The Siris followed a classic path: from enjoying the outdoors to working for its protection. "I suppose those early trips brought us into contact with Mother Nature and all her good and bad things," says Will, "and it just grew from there." He almost immediately got involved in the Sierra Club at the highest levels. He served on its board of directors for many years in the 1950s and 1960s and was its president for eight. He campaigned to keep dams out of the Grand Canyon, chainsaws out of the redwoods, and clear cuts out of the North Cascades. On the anti-Brower side in the 1960s schism, he counts David Brower's departure as one of his successes.

Jean Siri's activity found a local focus. After learning the ropes in the usual way—by attending meetings and watching the system at work—she took on a series of campaigns involving crucial pieces of the Bay shore. "I was trying to take the kids to the water," she remembers, "and I couldn't get to the Bay. And it made me mad." That Point Isabel and Brooks Island in Richmond are public parks today is largely her doing.

Will Siri at home in El Cerrito, 1997

But maybe the most satisfying of these successes was the one at Point Pinole.

Point Pinole is a green, triangular peninsula sticking out into San Pablo Bay north of the Richmond–San Rafael Bridge. It was long the site of an explosives factory and so had been left undeveloped. When that use ended in 1960, the land was purchased by Bethlehem Steel, with a major plant in mind. Tipped off by a reporter, Jean Siri says, "I went out to see what we were missing. And I fell in love with the place. And I thought, this is ridiculous, to give this up."

Acting before the steel plant plan made headlines, Siri sought ammunition from the state. "I went to California Resources Secretary Hugo Fisher, and I told him about this place that would make such a superb state park, and I just went on and on and on. I didn't tell him it belonged to Bethlehem Steel! So he sent one of the guys from State Parks down to survey it. He did a wonderful survey about what a wonderful park it would be."

When the coin dropped about the ownership, the state's interest waned. "But I had this wonderful survey. I just got people organized around it, and we won." Faced with bad public relations and shaky economics, the company sold the land to the East Bay Regional Park District in 1971.

Jean Siri's attention also turned at this time to pollution and toxic waste. Her interest was kindled when her frail father, visiting from out of town, fell ill from inhaling fumes from the Stauffer chemical plant. "I went to the air pollution board and studied them and studied the staff, and studied where all their weaknesses were, and their penchant in favor of industry, every time."

In the 1970s, Jean began working with the African American community in North Richmond, adjacent to the huge Chevron refinery. "I taught them all I knew about air pollution, and I took them over to meetings. They talked about their children who had asthma, and how much cancer there was, and all that." It was one of the first efforts nationally in the field now known as environmental justice. "So we started the West County Toxics Coalition. Now they travel all over the country, teaching other people from other minority communities how to do it.

"Then I decided to see how it would be to sit on a commission or a board and make decisions instead of standing out in the audience berating them." She ran first for the board of a sanitary district and then for city council in her town of El Cerrito, serving twice as mayor. Then she was elected to the board of the East Bay Regional Park District, whose holdings she had done so much to increase. She finds this post a delightful change from years of high pressure debate. "Everything they do is so nice. Everybody loves it."

Despite their accomplishments, the Siris are frankly pessimistic about the problems facing the planet and its people. Will hopes that young scientists will consider the consequences of their research more carefully than his generation did. Back then, he says, the attitude was: "We have this problem in the laboratory, let's see if we can find a solution. If I were growing up now with the interest I had in science, I would definitely [be concerned] by what else is going on in the world."

"Here's the only advice I have for young people," Jean says. "If you see something that should be remedied, that you think something should be done about, do it, for heaven's sakes."

Jean Siri at home in El Cerrito, 1997

Florence and Philip LaRiviere

—✐—

It began, you might say, with a picnic.

In the summer of 1952, recently moved from foggy Berkeley to sunny Palo Alto, Florence and Philip LaRiviere sought coolness on the bay shore. "There was an old, half broken-down picnic table down by the Palo Alto harbormaster's house," Florence says. "That was the end of the road. Everything was pickleweed and cordgrass beyond that point. And a marsh at evening is really lovely. You'd think it would be a real quiet place, but it's not, it's full of bird sounds, breezes blowing in the grasses. We just got very fond of it. We began wondering what on earth those birds were with the red legs and the black necks." So the couple joined the Audubon Society and learned much more than the identity of black-necked stilts.

Active in local Audubon in those days in the 1950s were two women named Harriet Mundy and Lucy Evans. Theirs were among the first voices raised anywhere around the Bay in opposition to fill and wetland development. Evans and Mundy led a campaign that, by 1963, persuaded Palo Alto to protect the strip of marshy bay front within its jurisdiction. The LaRivieres, busy with four children and two jobs, had a supporting role. "We knew those women," Florence says. "We used to go to the meetings, just to back them up. And that's how we started learning about what you say to convince political bodies that the lands they have are special."

In 1965, Florence read a newspaper blurb inviting people to a meeting about saving South Bay wetlands. She went, and heard Arthur Ogilvie, a Santa Clara County planner, propose a grand idea: the creation of a National Wildlife Refuge on both shores of the Bay. Ogilvie had the ear of a local congressman, Don Edwards, who thought he could make the miracle happen—given a wave of citizen support. In the ensuing five-year campaign, the LaRivieres helped to build that wave. In 1972, Congress proclaimed the San Francisco Bay National Wildlife Refuge—the first such area to be located in the heart of a metropolitan region.

The new refuge consisted partly of marshes, but mostly of diked ponds where Leslie Salt extracted salt from bay water. Such ponds are bird habitats in themselves, and the refuge advocates had no objection to salt harvest continuing, at least for the time being. The LaRivieres protested, however, when an agreement was struck that allowed salt production to go on, without much government oversight, for as long as the company chose.

As development crowded in closer around the

Florence and Philip LaRiviere at the Baylands Nature Preserve, Palo Alto, 2001 southern Bay, citizens rallied again, this time under the banner of the Citizens Committee to Complete the Refuge. Its goal: the expansion of the reserve to include just about every remaining salt pond or wetland scrap south of the Hayward–San Mateo Bridge. In 1988, at the urging of Don Edwards, Congress broadened the boundaries as requested, opening the way to purchase and preservation. Since then the committee has worked doggedly to translate authorization into reality. A major piece fell into place in 2002, when fifteen thousand more acres of South Bay salt ponds (now owned by Cargill) passed into public ownership.

Philip, a physicist by trade, has become a gadfly in his own right. He takes a special and critical interest in salt marsh restoration, in which dikes are broken to rewater dried-out areas behind them. If this is done right, marsh vegetation will quickly reappear. There are numerous ways, LaRiviere explains, to do it wrong. A common error is to make the opening to open water too small, so that tides within can't rise and fall in the full normal range. For complex reasons, this can delay the reestablishment of a functioning marsh or even prevent it entirely.

"But may I show you something good?" asks Philip. He pulls out a photo of a green expanse threaded with silver channels. "This is *our* marsh."

The site lies at the doorstep of the Don Edwards San Francisco Bay National Wildlife Refuge headquarters at the Coyote Hills in Fremont. It started out as an abandoned salt harvest area, a dry, white, sterile flat. Experts wondered whether anything could grow there. And indeed, when water was first reintroduced in the 1970s, nothing much did grow. But in 1986 the connection to the Bay was widened, letting more tidewater in. Ancient powers stirred. Cordgrass and then pickleweed appeared and spread. The California clapper rail, an endangered wetland-dependent bird, found the spot to its liking. In 1997, the former industrial site known as Tract 21 received its new name: the Florence and Philip LaRiviere Marsh.

Dwight Steele

—⌇—

As a labor lawyer in the 1940s, representing management, Dwight Steele spent many hours sitting across the table from Harry Bridges, the legendary leader of the International Longshore Workers Union. "I negotiated with him year after year after year. He said he had learned that no matter how bleak things look, when you are in a corner, you keep punching. And most of the time you'll land a lucky punch."

That was one of several lessons that Steele brought with him when he decided late in life to phase out his law practice and become a full-time environmental activist.

Born in Alameda in 1914, son of an engineer who specialized in dam construction, Steele got his first exposure to the out-of-doors on car camping trips to the Sierra. He fell in love with Lake Tahoe at a time when you could camp almost anywhere in the basin—even, as a car breakdown dictated one night, right beside the road at famous Emerald Bay.

In 1931, while Steele was attending the University of California at Berkeley, his father got him a seasonal job surveying dam sites in the northern Sierra Nevada. "So I spent all summer in these beautiful canyons of the Feather River. And I came home and said, 'You can't build dams there. You'll ruin the place!'" This did not, he recalls, go over well.

Steele's turn to activism came much later, however, after many years as a lawyer in the Hawaiian Islands.

Returning to California with his family in 1959, he reconnected to Lake Tahoe, where the family built a house in 1964. It was not the place he remembered. A casino-building boom was giving the lake an urban imprint; the clear mountain air was growing smoggy; and the lake water was steadily losing its world-famous dazzling clarity.

Beginning in 1968, Steele threw himself into the effort to halt the Tahoe Basin's environmental decline, working through the Sierra Club and the League to Save Lake Tahoe, which he chaired. Offered a position on the board of the Tahoe Regional Planning Agency, he took it only to resign in a very public protest against the agency's toothlessness. By 1980, with the bistate Regional Compact, California and Nevada at last began some serious regulation of development in the basin. The deterioration, though, is hard to arrest. "Whether we will be able to reverse what's going on is still problematical."

At home in the Bay Area, Steele put equal energy into the fight to stop the filling of San Francisco Bay. In 1969, the original Bay Conservation and Development Commission had finished its initial plan and was slated to go out of business—unless the legislature decided to make the body permanent. "I did a lot of lobbying," Steele recalls. "I didn't think of it as lobbying at the time, but I talked to a lot of assemblymen and senators, and worked very closely with Assemblyman John

Knox from Richmond, the author of a bill. It got to the point where occasionally he would call me and say 'We got a problem with Standard Oil, they want some exception or something; can you talk to them?' So I learned fairly quickly that I didn't have to be bashful about making an impact."

A later project of Steele's is also his favorite, he says, because the results are so tangible. This is the creation, on eight miles of bay front between Berkeley and Richmond, of the Eastshore State Park. Former railroad land, this strip was slated for massive development; one plan called for nine waterfront high rises. Working with Sylvia McLaughlin and others in Citizens for East Shore Parks, Steele set out to persuade the owners to sell and the state to buy. A lifetime of skills came into play. "I set up meetings back in the late '80s with the top [railroad] people. We said from the outset that we are not here to beat you over the head but just to help you reach the conclusion that it's in the best interests of the shareholders of your corporation not to develop this property but to sell it to the state."

It took a change of corporate ownership, but finally the company (now Catellus) became a willing seller. The park is a reality.

As a lawyer, Steele knows the value of doing one's homework. He will spend ten hours, on occasion, preparing a three-minute speech. He preaches, too, the values of precision and restraint in argument. "In my environmental work I've been very careful not to talk about something I don't know about. And not to exaggerate. Other people, even people who have the opposite view, developers, have said to me and publicly that we can trust Dwight, whatever he says. And that takes a long time to develop."

Again, he absorbed the virtue, not of compromise exactly, but of understanding. "One of the things you learn in negotiating is that you don't impose your views on the other side. You have to find a way to accommodate the basic needs and objectives of the opposition as well as your own. So you learn to be sensitive to where the other side is coming from and what is possible."

Dwight Steele at Cesar Chavez Park at the shore of the Bay in Berkeley, 1997

Bill Davoren

—ɯɯ—

The defenders of San Francisco Bay had won a great victory in 1969, yet all was not well with the object of their concern. Even as bay fill slowed and stopped, it became apparent that the system was biologically in trouble and that this trouble stemmed from causes far outside the control of the new Bay Conservation and Development Commission.

The Bay is, after all, not just an arm of the sea. It is an estuary, a mixing zone of salt water and fresh, the recipient of rivers from the heart of California. Runoff from the snows of Mount Shasta and the heights of the central Sierra is destined for the Golden Gate via the Sacramento and San Joaquin Rivers. But in the twentieth century, as dams were built and ever more water drawn off for agriculture and cities, the flow of these streams weakened, and the quality of water coming down them worsened.

Anadromous fish like salmon and steelhead—creatures that spend much of their lives at sea but make their way up inland streams to spawn—were the first to suffer the effects. In the 1970s a marked decline in the spawning runs began. In the 1980s decline became collapse.

Early in that decade, at a time when the Save San Francisco Bay Association had settled into what some saw as a complacent role, a new gadfly came on the scene. He was determined to show the world that "saving the Bay" meant saving the watershed, too. His name was Bill Davoren.

Davoren started life in Denver, where his grandfather had helped to establish the city's park system. (In a nice coincidence, Sylvia McLaughlin's father later managed those parks, but the families were unacquainted.) After graduating from the University of Colorado in 1949, he spent the 1950s as a job-hopping journalist, publicist, and Democratic Party activist. In 1960 he became an advisor to President Kennedy's secretary of the interior, Stewart Udall. As a kind of roving planner for the southwestern states, he came to see clearly what dams and diversions were doing to rivers and fish around the West in general, and to the Sacramento and San Joaquin Rivers, San Francisco Bay's great feeder streams, in particular.

In 1966, the new Bay Conservation and Development Commission set up shop across the street from Davoren's San Francisco office. He got to know Mel Lane and Joe Bodovitz and became known at BCDC as "the friendly fed." Notably he helped the Bay agency deal with the powerful Army Corps of Engineers on dredging issues.

Bill Davoren at his waterfront home in Tiburon, 2004

In 1973, when Lane and Bodovitz had moved on to the California Coastal Commission, Bodovitz telephoned: "Bill, can we borrow you?" Davoren spent three years on the commission staff, helping the new body through the formative period. He advised on the San Onofre nuclear power plant issue and had the satisfaction of seeing strong language about anadromous fish inserted in the first California Coastal Plan. But of course the fate of most of those fish would be determined inland, not in the coastal zone.

Davoren's last post in government was with the federal Fish and Wildlife Service. Here he tried to draw scientists and policy people together to focus on the problems of the Bay as related to those of the watershed. Unable to make this synthesis work inside the federal bureaucracy, in 1981 he stepped outside it to found a private organization, The Bay Institute of San Francisco. It is part think tank and part advocate, and its approach might be summed up in Davoren's slogan: "Save a River for the Bay!"

Davoren founded the institute for another and very specific reason. The ultimate authority in California water matters, the State Water Resources Control Board, had finally declared that it had the right and the duty to set guaranteed levels of freshwater inflow for the Bay. A battle royal was impending. The Bay Institute—the newest kid on the environmental block, without an office, without a budget, without lawyers, almost without a staff—announced that it would be a full participant.

The actual start of hearings before the board was long delayed. In the interim, in 1984 The Bay Institute raised the alarm about another watershed issue: the pollution disaster at Kesterson National Wildlife Refuge near the San Joaquin River, where agricultural drain water polluted with selenium was killing birds.

When the water hearings finally got going in 1987, three great interest groups—agriculture, urban water districts, and environmentalists—locked horns. Davoren covered developments in a tabloid newsletter called *Bay on Trial*. Soon the process bogged down, but the exhausted opponents had no choice but to keep talking. Negotiations culminated finally in 1994 in a patched-together document called the Bay-Delta Accord, to which The Bay Institute was a key signatory.

Though fully satisfactory to no party, the Bay-Delta Accord opened new possibilities for the future of the Bay and its upstream anteroom, the Sacramento–San Joaquin River Delta. The accord brought into being CALFED, an uneasy alliance of state and federal government agencies that is trying to work out ways of meeting California's water needs without doing further harm to ecosystems. The agreement permitted the needs of fish to trump, at times, the needs of water users. And it promised to unlock large sums of money for ecological restoration, including the rewatering of thousands of acres of dried-out former marshlands.

What the accord did not do was the very thing Davoren had sought from the beginning. It did not set, and guarantee, specific levels of freshwater inflow to the Bay.

Now retired, Bill Davoren continues to speak out for stronger, clearer solutions. "I yearn for something firm and positive," he says. "We're still diddling around."

Lois Crozier-Hogle

It starts, for many people, with a place: one well-loved landscape, an experiential turf, an imprint on the brain, that later seems the source of commitment to the wild things of the world. For Lois Crozier-Hogle the place was Huntington Lake in the Sierra: "the streams and the rocks, big rocks that you could climb on, and the trees, and the meadows. I remember gathering strawberries the size of your little fingernail, in a glass. They were red, they were the fruit of the time, from these meadows. And watching water beetles, water snakes, in the pools."

The seed planted in childhood stayed dormant for a while. At the University of Redlands in southern California in the 1930s, Crozier-Hogle was involved with social, not environmental causes. She was part of a leftist Christian group that organized the recall of a corrupt mayor of Los Angeles. "I think all colleges should do that for their students," she says. "Radicalize them. I got the idea that the world needed to be saved, and I was out to do it.

"I didn't know I was an environmentalist. I didn't know it until I got here and saw these foothills."

"Here" was Palo Alto, and the "foothills" were the darkly forested eastward faces of the Santa Cruz Mountains. Arriving in 1959 after years in New York and England, Crozier-Hogle went through several stages of falling in love with the landscape—and learning with alarm what was about to happen to it.

In the late 1950s, cities up and down the Peninsula were expanding as fast as they could do the paperwork of annexation. The flatlands along the Bay were occupied. The steep, slide-prone mountains were next in line. In Palo Alto, some citizens sought to protect the nearby hills by electing sympathetic people to the city council. Losing in this effort, the group disbanded. Crozier-Hogle kept pressing one of the leaders to reactivate the movement, "because I thought it shouldn't die. He said, 'I'm tired, you do it!' So I got together twenty-six people, and we started the Committee for Green Foothills. It was named that night, May 10, 1962."

Throwing herself into the work of the Foothills committee, she built it into a force that could fight off intrusions into the mountains along a front line fifty miles long. She learned the power of sheer persistence. She also learned the power of information, of simply doing one's homework. "One time I heard a planning commissioner say, 'We depend upon the Committee for Green Foothills to give us information that we don't have. We can depend on it, it's accurate.'"

Over the decades, Crozier-Hogle has seen a lot of evolution in the attitudes of the public and political leaders alike. "When we started," she says, "we were just beginning to educate people about the environment. Today, most of our Santa Clara supervisors are environmentally knowledgeable." When a bit of a reminder

is required, the committee and its allies are ready to turn out in force.

When she began her activism, Crozier-Hogle was a member of the species *conservationist*. When the term *environmentalist* gained currency, around 1970, she adopted it gladly. "'Conservationist' reminds me of being conservative. And I am anything but that. 'Environmentalist' says what it is."

Looking back on a long life, Crozier-Hogle is not without regrets. During the peak of her land-saving activity, she rarely walked those hills she was fighting for. "It was one phone call after another, meetings, meetings in the evening, doing desk work, and having my children turn somersaults when they wanted attention, when I was on the phone. I gave my whole life to it. It was not so good, actually. I think the smart women were the ones who took the weekends off for their families."

It may have been a growing disquiet, as well as her environmentalism, that led her to study Native American traditions, where she found a "golden thread" of sensitivity and equilibrium. Her book *Surviving in Two Worlds: Contemporary Native American Voices* appeared in 1997. "One of the things I learned from the Indians is balance. That life needs to be in balance. For me, there wasn't enough focusing on the inner. I was a victim, you might say, of all kinds of outer influences coming in all the time. They were so fascinating, so interesting, that I couldn't say 'No.' I needed to say 'No' a lot earlier."

The No imposed itself in 1999, when she suffered a stroke. Even as she worked to recover her health, Lois Crozier-Hogle took it as a lesson. "I feel quieter," she says. "I was a stony heart, I think. But now that's all changed.

"I think maybe that is what I am heading for, to try to do. To catch the meaning in life. I have found a lot, but I think there is more."

Lois Crozier-Hogle in her garden in Palo Alto, 1997

Olive Mayer

—m—

When Olive Hendricks was a little girl in New Jersey in the 1930s, she played with chemicals in her parents' garage. "I took sulfur and potassium nitrate and I wrapped it up in silver foil from a Hershey bar. I'd put it on the concrete and bang it with a hammer. And it was like a firecracker; it would go BAM! So I made one a little bigger. And one day I cracked the concrete, and that was the end of that!"

Her next hobby was collecting butterflies. "We went hiking," Mayer says, "and went looking for the bushes where we would find the butterflies and caterpillars. I had the cages in my bedroom, and they made their chrysalises. Then we let them all go."

From gunpowder to lepidoptera. Years later, Mayer made a change in her life that echoed that early transition. She had meanwhile earned a B.S. in engineering from Swarthmore College, married, and moved out west. In 1945 she was running a machine shop in Palo Alto. World War II was over, but the demand for weapons showed no sign of abating. "All the jobs that I could get were for war, in one way or another. They were so busy building atom bombs. So I said, if they are going to fight their damn wars, they are going to do it without me." She switched to making science materials for schools.

In 1968, after twenty-five years in business, Mayer closed up shop for good. After a trip around the world with her husband, Henry, she rediscovered in the hills of San Mateo County the pursuits of her youth. She started hiking.

"This is one of the most beautiful places in the whole world," she says. "Gorgeous meadows, flowers, trees, redwoods. I decided that I was going to teach other people about the trails and get people to appreciate this land that we have." Kids especially. "They don't even know the names of the trees or the names of the streams in the county," Mayer says with indignation. "They don't know the geography of the place where they live!"

Working initially through the Girl Scouts, Mayer was soon escorting youngsters down Peninsula trails, forming friendships with other leaders, and sharing the realization that these landscapes were vulnerable. "And when a place that we loved was about to be destroyed, we decided that we couldn't allow that and we had to do something with this damn government down here! We've got to make them appreciate what's going on in their backyard."

Of the many campaigns Mayer threw herself into, one was huge: the thirty-year effort to block what could have been an eight-lane freeway down the San

Olive Mayer at San Gregorio State Beach, 1997

Mateo coast. "I thought, nobody would want that freeway; the coast is so beautiful," Mayer says. "But everybody was so busy building their homes and getting their children educated and taking care of the schools and all the things people have to do in life, that nobody was thinking about the coast except the developers. They had big plans, believe me." And the San Mateo County government fully supported those plans.

Initially, Mayer remembers, the opposition consisted "just of myself and a couple of people from the coast. We never thought whether we were going to win or not; we were just going to keep working. One step at a time. And we did. We foiled the freeway builders at every step. We followed everything they tried to do, and we blocked them."

Finally, after many twists, the issue boiled down to the question of what to do about Devil's Slide. This was a stretch of the northern San Mateo coast where the narrow existing highway, carved into an ancient landslide, would crumble toward the sea whenever prolonged winter rains saturated the ground. The state wanted to replace the troublesome road with an inland

bypass, in which opponents saw the germ of the hated freeway. Mayer and her allies pushed for an alternative: a tunnel, which would solve the stability problem while all but foreclosing future expansion. In 1998, by a margin of three to one, the San Mateo County electorate locked in the tunnel plan. Construction began in 2005.

Mayer ponders the lessons of the experience. "I believe that the government is only going to move when it is pushed by a large number of people. Without that it's not going to do anything. Whether you want clean air or cleanup of some pollution or radiation or stopping logging in a certain place—nothing is going to happen unless a large number of people raise hell. That's what I learned."

In her own life Mayer made the transition, step by step, from enjoying the natural world to teaching about it to working for its preservation. She thinks it is vital to keep this pathway open. "The joy that I have had in my lifetime, in climbing the mountains and exploring these hills and walking on the beach, walking these trails! I don't want that to die in the world; I want it to continue. I want other people to enjoy it too."

Eleanor Boushey

Eleanor Boyd started life in a tiny southern Arizona mining town with wild desert for playground. She was supposed to stay inside a fence her mine manager father built to keep rattlesnakes out, but the barrier couldn't keep Eleanor and her two younger brothers in. "We used to climb over the fence and walk in the hills; that was our favorite thing to do," says Boushey. "I just loved the open space and the feeling of no one having been there. And that stayed all my life."

In 1927, Eleanor's family left the bony hills of Tucson for the greener slopes of the San Francisco Peninsula. Two years later she enrolled in Stanford University. "She was a campus queen," notes friend and fellow conservationist Allan Brown. "She was a member of one of the very popular sororities, and she was very attractive, and she had all these guys at her feet! You wouldn't think she would turn out to be a very strong environmentalist, but she did."

In an alphabetically seated history class, Eleanor found herself next to a young man named Homer Boushey, with whom she fell in love. Soon married, the couple moved back East. But the new Mrs. Boushey kept up on events in the state she regarded as her real home. "I used to read about what was happening in California, the destruction of open space here. And I thought, if I ever get back to California, that is what I am going to try to do something about."

In 1961, Eleanor and Homer bought a house a few miles outside Palo Alto, in a woodsy suburban region that wasn't officially a town and didn't especially want to be one. But the highway engineers were knocking on its door with a plan for an expressway climbing the escarpment of the Santa Cruz Mountains to link up with Skyline Boulevard along the crest. To resist that, the community had to organize. Both the Bousheys started going to meetings.

Out of this community resistance grew a plan to create a town of Portola Valley. In 1964, an election was scheduled to ratify the idea and to choose a first town council.

When the organizers phoned the Boushey home one night, it was Homer they asked for and invited to run. As Eleanor recalls, "He said, 'No, I won't do it because I get too angry.' But he handed me the phone, and I said, 'I think I'll run,' and they said, 'Oh.'" Women in government were a rarity in those days. But run she did, and was narrowly elected—put over the top, she likes to claim, by the votes of Homer's mother and her friends at a local retirement home.

The new town council made it clear that the community did not want the state's proposed road, and the California Division of Highways (as it then was called) backed off.

Boushey stayed on the Portola Valley council for fourteen years and served three terms as mayor. "She was the voice of conservation," council colleague Bob

Brown (brother of Allan) remembers. "She was always urging us to take stands on every environmental issue, sometimes beyond Portola Valley." She was also, he adds, a consensus builder. "She mothered the council a little."

Boushey retired from the council only when she was sure that another woman was running for the post. Her reasons for this go beyond loyalty to gender. "Women who run for city government are usually independent. But the men, they have some financial tie-up somewhere to a real estate company or something." She cautions women against being too easily discouraged. "I think they take it personally if they aren't elected. It's silly; you have to be willing to lose sometimes."

As a council member and on her own time, Boushey kept working to preserve the Santa Cruz Mountains. She formed an enduring friendship with Lois Crozier-Hogle, founder of the Committee for Green Foothills. She learned ins and outs of Sacramento politicking from Helen Reynolds of the California Roadside Council. She served on a state committee for scenic highways and saw her beloved Skyline Boulevard become the second California State Scenic Highway in 1968.

As a conservationist in Portola Valley, Eleanor Boushey has an awful lot of company. (No less than eight people profiled in this book live in this one small town.) It's a chicken and egg question: Does the environment shape the environmentalist here, or the other way around? Boushey tends to think that place comes first. "They settle here because they like the open space," she says. "And then they find there is a movement they can help."

Since Boushey's retirement, the town has remained resistant to large-scale development. On some occasions the secret weapon seems to be the same one that Boushey claims got her elected: a large turnout from the local retirement home. "A legislative body just can't take action against a big audience," she notes. "They just psychologically can't."

Eleanor Boushey at home in Portola Valley, 1997

Lennie Roberts

Growing up in the East Bay village of Orinda, Lennie Roberts says, "I used to look out and imagine that I owned a meadow I could see across the valley. It was really owned by the East Bay Municipal Utility District. I used to call that my meadow."

She puts her finger on a feeling quite fundamental to the conservationist mind: that public lands don't just belong to the government, or to some abstract People, but to each of us as an individual.

That meadow was one of her imprints. Another was her family's ranch in Mendocino County, where she went in summer, swimming and riding horseback and helping her uncle pick apples. It was that ranch that got her started, in the seventh grade, as a letter-writing activist. "Nearby there was a beautiful old-growth grove of redwoods called the Hendy Woods," Roberts recalls. "In the period of time when all of Mendocino was being logged, these trees were too big for the saws they were using to cut them, so they had not cut this particular grove of trees."

Now, in the middle 1940s, a new wave of logging was at hand, with far more effective tools. "So I wrote a letter to Governor Earl Warren and asked him to do whatever he could to save Hendy Woods. Five days later, he sent me a letter back, which of course you never get today—a personal letter back saying he shared my love of the redwoods and he would send my letter on to the head of the State Parks Department and that he hoped they would be saved. And indeed the Hendy Woods were saved, and they are now a state park."

Later, while studying at Stanford University, Roberts spent a lot of time in the Sierra Nevada, often at the Sierra Club's Clair Tappaan Lodge near Donner Summit. "So I was just adventuring and enjoying all these things," she says, "not doing something about them." After her marriage, though, she moved to Ladera, a small community outside Palo Alto. There, at a garden club, she heard a talk by Lois Crozier-Hogle of the Committee for Green Foothills. "I thought that's great, and I want to be doing something more than writing letters for a garden club; I think I'd like to get involved with that organization."

By 1968 she was on the committee's board of directors. She was also part of the group that pushed for formation of a local government entity to buy open space in the Santa Cruz Mountains. The Midpeninsula Regional Open Space District was created by a public vote in 1972. A 1976 campaign to extend its reach to San Mateo County put Roberts, for

Lennie Roberts at Jasper Ridge Biological Preserve in Palo Alto, 1997

the first time, into a public role. "Up until then I had thought that if I ever had to stand up and speak in front of anybody—the board of supervisors, for example—something terrible would happen. So I just decided, well, okay, the way you can do this and not go through the floor is to get so knowledgeable about what you are talking about that nobody can ask you a question that you cannot answer." In 1978, she joined the staff of the Committee for Green Foothills as its legislative advocate for San Mateo County.

Roberts used her new-found skills in three initiative campaigns that have served to keep the coastal part of San Mateo County—"the Coastside"—out of the urban sphere.

The first came in 1986 and was born of frustration with the San Mateo board of supervisors. The balance of opinion on that body having tilted, for a time, in favor of development, the board sought to weaken the protection of the Coastside in what is called the Local Coastal Plan. "So we decided that we would put an initiative measure on the ballot that would enact thirty-eight policies from our Coastal Plan. And if the voters enacted them, we would also provide that they could not be weakened unless the voters approved in the

future." With the help of a private donor who funded a professional campaign, the protective policies got a resounding endorsement. "Measure A passed by 63 percent. And it really changed the politics about the coast. Since 1986 the board of supervisors doesn't try to go against the voters."

The second key electoral fight was over an initiative offered by developers, who sought an exception from the Coastal Plan to allow a major project near Half Moon Bay. This time the open space advocates were outspent by more than ten to one, but increased their majority to a stunning 82 percent.

In the third initiative, in 1998, the voters decided how to reroute the Coast Highway past the unstable Devil's Slide. By choosing a tunnel of limited capacity, they foreclosed any future freeway down the San Mateo coastline.

Almost imperceptibly, Lennie Roberts has found herself becoming what she never would have dreamed of being: a power. In the mid-1990s, a local newspaper asked the board of supervisors which of the people they dealt with were most influential. "The two people they identified," says Roberts with a laugh, "were the county manager and me!"

Robert Praetzel

One of the glories of the Bay Area is its Golden Gate, entrance to one of the world's great harbors, site of one of the world's great bridges, and centerpiece of one of the world's great parks, the Golden Gate National Recreation Area. Both shores of the strait are open, inviting, and protected; and the rugged Marin shore is the start of a coastal greenbelt that runs north for fifty increasingly wild miles. Local people, tramping these trails, enjoying these views, take the gift for granted. Few now remember the campaign to create the park and how hard it was to keep the U.S. Army, former master of these shores, from selling them off to the highest bidder. Fewer still remember the improbable episode of Marincello.

Marincello was a planned city of twenty thousand people that would have occupied the heart of the Marin Headlands, one ridge north of the Golden Gate, adjacent to the Army lands. It was the dream of a man named Thomas Frouge, who believed in building self-sufficient "new towns" as an alternative to sprawling suburban development. This was and remains an intriguing idea, but an odd one for this site, much too close to San Francisco to attain the desired self-sufficiency. It was that propinquity that attracted Frouge's backer, the land development division of Gulf Oil.

Twenty thousand people in the headlands? Twenty apartment towers? A hilltop hotel? An Avenue of the Flags? Walk the gentle trails of the headlands today,

watch the fogs flow in and out, and it seems fantastical.

Yet the project once seemed a done deal. Swayed by a sophisticated sales campaign, the Marin County board of supervisors had approved the plan with token modifications. Long-standing policies had been amended to accommodate it. Surveyors' stakes had sprouted, marking future boulevards. And in the swale called Tennessee Valley, where hikers now shrug on their packs for the stroll to an astonishingly wild shore, there rose a pair of stucco gatehouses: the portals of Marincello.

That Marincello does not exist today is the doing of a small, embattled band of local lawyers. Two of them, Martin Rosen and Doug Ferguson, went on to full-time careers in conservation. The third, Robert Praetzel, settled for one big victory. His contribution, his cohorts say, was absolutely key.

Soon after the development was approved, opponents from neighboring communities circulated a petition to require a countywide referendum on the project. When the county clerk invalidated just enough signatures to cause the petition to fail, the opponents sued. In a second, parallel suit, they argued that the authorities had cut several procedural corners in their rush toward approving Marincello.

Peripherally aware of these goings-on, Praetzel knew which side he was rooting for. Conservation ran in his family. His mother-in-law was Mary Donnelly, a long-time leader in the Marin Conservation League; his wife, Nancy, was an activist in her own right. He himself had represented clients arrested for lying down in front of logging trucks in West Marin. But Marincello was not at the top of his list. He lived in Kentfield, too far away from the development to take the threat personally; and he was quite sufficiently busy.

Then he got a call from a friend in Sausalito, one of the architects of the two lawsuits, named Bob Conn. Pressure had been brought. Conn had learned that his job was at risk if he persevered. Could Praetzel help? He enthusiastically agreed, joining his colleague Martin Rosen on a reconstituted legal team. Rosen and later Douglas Ferguson handled the case about the petition; Praetzel carried the procedural suit, the one pointing to errors in the approval process. To this day he bristles at the charge that these points were technicalities. "The technicality was the fact that they didn't follow the law."

A judge warned Frouge and Gulf that they proceeded at their own risk: anything built might literally have to be torn down. Meanwhile, the development partnership was undergoing the financial strains common to big projects. It is hard to know which factor was decisive. But the fact is that, after 1967, no more work was done at Marincello.

For the next four years only legal paper moved.

The California Supreme Court declined to second-guess the county clerk on the disputed signatures. Things looked grim for the opponents, but then a State Court of Appeals ruled on the remaining procedural case, accepting Praetzel's argument that the supervisors had omitted essential steps in their haste to act. The approval of Marincello was void. The applicants could bring the plan forward again, of course, but in a far less complaisant climate of opinion. "By that time," says Praetzel, "the whole attitude had changed."

In the end, Gulf withdrew and sold the land to The Nature Conservancy, which held it until the National Park Service had the money to purchase the property in turn. Today it is a vital link in the vast Golden Gate National Recreation Area.

For Doug Ferguson and Martin Rosen, the Marincello battle was a turning point, giving their lives a new direction as professional environmentalists. For Bob Praetzel, it was an adventure not to be repeated, at least on the same scale. As a kind of citizen soldier, he had stepped forward on one key issue, donated over a thousand hours, and seen it happily resolved. For the time being, that sufficed.

With retirement, however, Robert Praetzel is reengaging. Among other things, he is working with Huey Johnson to regenerate the state's salmon runs by restoring streams and securing water for fish.

Robert Praetzel at the Marin Headlands site once slated for Marincello, now part of the Golden Gate National Recreational Area, 2000

Douglas Ferguson

—ɯɯ—

There are two things I'm pretty good at," says lawyer and land-saver Douglas Ferguson of Mill Valley. "I can help you raise money, and I can help you solve seemingly insolvable problems. That is the thrill of it."

Studying law at Stanford in the early 1960s, Ferguson was a long way from feeling any thrill. Courses were geared toward corporate practice, where the money was. The idea of "public interest" lawyering was as yet scarcely heard of. Ferguson felt something missing in the trade he was assiduously mastering.

Then he and his wife, Jane, moved to Sausalito and found a battle going on in their new backyard. With a start, Ferguson realized that his training had given him the means to change the outcome—if he chose.

Like much of the floor of San Francisco Bay and its various inlets, Richardson Bay off Sausalito was officially private property, sold off by the California Legislature soon after statehood. Now a company had bought up the underwater lots and announced its plans to fill the area and build a hotel. Local people were upset, but could the plan be stopped? It was, after all, private land.

"I said, 'Hey, you can't build in the bay!' and people said, 'I think he can; he owns these underwater streets.' I said, 'That's just crazy. You shouldn't be able to build on underwater streets. There must be a rule—I'll go to the law books.' So I did, and what do you know?"

What Ferguson found in the books was an ancient doctrine concerning what is called the public trust for fishing and navigation. According to this legal teaching, regarded back then as obscure, submerged lands are never private property in the fullest sense. You can own them, all right, but you cannot so change them that other people cannot fish there or take boats across the overlying water. What is wet must stay wet. Its spine stiffened by this knowledge, the Sausalito city council refused the hotel application, and the project disappeared.

At that point, Ferguson admits, he was still really more interested in the legal doctrine involved than in the particular cause it served.

But it was not long after the Sausalito battle that Ferguson boarded a bus for San Francisco and found himself strap-hanging next to a fellow named Huey Johnson, the local head of an organization that Ferguson had never heard of, The Nature Conservancy. As they chatted, Johnson told him of a large and tricky land preservation deal that was pending in Wyoming. Some of what he heard set legal question marks

Douglas Ferguson at Richardson Bay, Mill Valley, 1997

jiggling in Ferguson's brain. "At just that point we got off the bus and sat down on the bus stop bench so I could explain to him about the Statute of Frauds."

One thing led to another, and soon Ferguson was doing pro bono legal work for the Conservancy. "Huey and I did some really wiggy deals, often to the initial upset (but eventual delight) of his superiors." About a year later, Johnson left the Conservancy to found his own organization, the Trust for Public Land. Ferguson joined the board of the Trust and sits on it still.

At about the time he met Johnson, Ferguson involved himself in the fight to stop the huge Marincello development near Sausalito. With fellow lawyers Robert Praetzel and Martin Rosen, he tied the plan up in the courts. Meanwhile, Johnson was talking to the would-be developer back East. "And the folks at Frouge Corporation said to Johnson, 'Well, you are telling us that our development is at risk and that we may lose these lawsuits. But we have every confidence that we are going to prevail. And in any event,' they said, 'we will wear these lawyers down on the other side. They are just three people working for nothing, you know.' And Huey, who is always a good person in a negotiation, apparently replied, 'I don't think you understand. I know those guys and you will never wear them down. They're crazy. They will go on forever!'"

The Nature Conservancy got the land.

Ferguson is troubled that land preservers are so often fighting for leftovers, trying to lessen the consequences of unwise land use decisions. "At the Trust for Public Land now we are doing significant land assemblages. We take a look at where development is and where development is going, and we think about preserving significant areas that will be buffers and green zones for development as it occurs, rather than just picking up the leftover scraps from the table. We are trying to sit at the table, helping to channel development down the appropriate corridor.

"As happens with many people," says Ferguson, "it was a hot issue in my own backyard that woke me up. But working with the Trust for Public Land, I understood that my backyard is all over the country. I go to Baltimore and I go to Georgia and I go to Connecticut, and I work with folks who are cleaning up *their* backyards, and I realize that they are also helping me clean up mine."

Martin Rosen

—⚏—

"We were the luckiest people ever born." This is the message Martin Rosen and his brother, growing up in Depression-era Los Angeles, got from their parents, loud and clear. Their father had reached the United States, a stowaway from Poland, in 1916; their mother fled to the New World after escaping a pogrom in Ukraine. After that, a mere economic downturn was no big deal. Grateful for a new life in a new country, the elder Rosens instilled in their children "an obligation to spread that luck."

Growing up, studying law, and starting a family in Marin County, Rosen wasn't sure what form that service would take. In his first formative battle, he was driven not so much by concern for the land as by sheer irritation at the arrogance of power.

That battle was over Marincello, the vast development proposed for the Marin Headlands in the mid-1960s by Gulf Oil and the Frouge Corporation. "They came in out of Pittsburgh in such an oppressive, seductive manner," says Rosen. "I got involved not so much for an environmental purpose as a civic purpose. I just felt it was terrible that these few people could turn around an entire landscape, and not even consult the people." With colleagues Robert Praetzel and Doug Ferguson, Rosen managed the lawsuits that doomed the project. It was a turning point for Marin County and a turning point for him.

As a result of this experience, Rosen went to work for Huey Johnson at The Nature Conservancy, and a few years later he followed Johnson to his new organization, the Trust for Public Land. In 1978, Rosen became the organization's president, a post he held for twenty years.

The trust specialized in tricky, sometimes unglamorous projects that more traditional land conservancies would not touch. It bought wild forest at Big Sur and weedy, polluted lots on the banks of the Los Angeles River, desert ranches and their precious water rights, even old buildings. It created the Martin Luther King Historic District in downtown Atlanta. It acquired a piece of the shore of Walden Pond in Massachusetts where high-rise buildings were planned. It helped the landless Nez Perce Indian tribe in eastern Oregon gain title to a large ranch. Rosen feels a creative zest in such deal-making. "Money not only talks," he says. "It also sings and dances."

Along the way, Rosen traveled a lot, and he thought a lot, sometimes in directions few of his fellow environmentalists pursue. Immersed as he was in the detail of law and land, he remained at heart a generalist, "Jeffersonian, not Thoreauvian."

Rosen has a bone to pick with colleagues who devote themselves to single issues and downgrade, sometimes explicitly, the importance of others. "You know the attitude," he says. "'Until we solve IT, everything else is sideshow, secondary.' To me, that kind of

intellectual arrogance is terminal." Not even world population growth, cited by many as the problem underlying all, deserves this status in his view.

Another big theme: The opponent of the moment must not be written off forever. "I've been a gunslinger. Winner takes all; loser takes nothing." But then what? "My approach always seeks to make allies out of adversaries, listening and learning and involving people in this cause. You have to not just educate them, you have to recruit them. Or their children. Or their wives, or their bosses or subordinates. Because unless and until we do, we will be talking to ourselves."

Nor should the environmentalist's concern shut off where human sufferings begin. The pure "green" focus, Rosen notes, "is attractive because it is less threatening. You don't have to worry about the social problems—you can look right past the terrible schools and the crappy health care system and the people stuck in poverty—we're beyond that! We're worried about biodiversity, so we don't have to get involved in all that other stuff. It's very attractive, very seductive. Because it's clean. Unrisky. Uncontroversial. Shortsighted. Wrong.

"We have to work with religions, with police departments, with taxpayer associations, with kids, with immigrants, with foundations, with businesses, that may not put the environment even on their screen—but who, if genuinely welcomed and treated with honor and dignity, will be our future." Seeking such "new sources of ignition," he has worked with Baptist churches, with convicts in prison, with the Garden Clubs of America, with tribes in British Columbia.

Issues are often more complex, Rosen adds, than advocates like them to appear. "We don't have pure, perfect solutions—ever! Whether you are talking about irradiated food or clinical tests or cloning or ferryboats. You have to get really close to the data and suffer the uncertainties, and allow for error, but at the same time go beyond paralysis. There are always many sides to be addressed and resolved. I live in dilemmas.

"People ask me whether I'm an optimist or a pessimist. Who cares? Who cares?

"Are you engaged or are you indifferent?

"If you're indifferent you're dying. If you are engaged, you're alive."

Martin Rosen at the Trust for Public Land office in San Francisco, 1997

Barbara Eastman

—ɯ—

There is a practical quality to Barbara Eastman. It doesn't surprise you to learn that she was once a dab hand with a drafter's pencil. It was early in World War II, in a quick course at the University of California, that she discovered this aptitude. "In half a day," Eastman says, "I learned how to draft, which is to draw pieces of machinery, that's the simplest way I can explain it. You draw the whole thing, and then you draw the parts to make it. And in the afternoon I went to the strength and materials laboratory to see what could be made. You didn't want to draw something that couldn't be made."

Later, pursuing the craft for the war effort, she got an apology from a supervisor who had assumed that a female draftsman could only be a beginner. "I'm awfully sorry," he said. "We didn't realize that you knew what you were doing."

More than one opponent of Eastman's in the conservation wars may well have had the same thought.

Born in 1918 in San Francisco, Barbara Eastman has lived most of her life in the South Bay, where she worked with the Committee for Green Foothills. She was one of the co-founders of the regional group Citizens for Regional Recreation and Parks (now the Greenbelt Alliance) and served a term on the board of the Bay Conservation and Development Commission.

But her name will always be linked to her second home, the native ground of her husband Bill: Inverness on the Point Reyes Peninsula in Marin County.

Time was when the hundred square miles of Point Reyes belonged to a single intermarried family, the Shafters and the Howards. When the vast estate broke up after World War II and the constituent dairy ranches were sold to their tenants, the real estate agent who handled the dissolution claimed as his commission the bit of the peninsula that locals most loved: a series of sheltered beaches on the forested west shore of Tomales Bay just north of the existing town. Development was planned.

In 1945, Eastman involved herself in the campaign to get the region set aside as a state park.

The state was not yet purchasing parks with public money, and the legislature was only willing to help those locals who would help themselves. To raise matching funds for the first key purchase, Shell Beach, Eastman and her friends "gave whist parties and we had cake bakes, all the traditional things. We were close to the deadline when the state was going to withdraw their offer to help." Then rescue came from Caroline Livermore of Kentfield, the godmother of Marin County conservation, who borrowed the needed funds.

Barbara Eastman at Tomales Bay in Inverness, 1999

It was in the cause of Tomales Bay State Park that Eastman, "a very private person," got over a long reluctance to speak out in public. It happened one night when she passed a stack of notes to a committee colleague, a San Francisco matron "who looked like she owned the Bank of England. And she said, 'Why are you giving this to me? You've done the work, you have to make the plea.'" Eastman did and soon found a positive pleasure in public speaking. She especially enjoys fielding the questions that often follow a formal presentation. "That's the most fun. Because then you don't have to think of how to convince them; you can just tell them the way it is. You can tell whether you have gotten across at all, what sort of questions have come up in people's minds."

Tomales Bay State Park was a warm-up for the campaign to secure for public use the huge remainder of Point Reyes. In the late 1950s, the National Park Service conducted a survey of the coasts of the United States to find what undeveloped segments might be purchased for the park system. Of the shockingly few candidates they found, the Point Reyes Peninsula— kept out of the swing of development by bad roads, fog, and the long reign of the Howard-Shafters—was the finest. When the study results were announced, a race began between the preservers and developers seeking, in their different ways, to cash in.

Eastman and her colleagues founded a Point Reyes National Seashore Foundation to lead the fight. "It was one step forward and two steps back for quite a while." Local opinion was divided, and the Marin County board of supervisors actually voted 3-2 to oppose the park. Congress proclaimed the seashore in 1962 but appropriated money late and stingily. For years the new park existed as a patchwork of unconnected parcels, with development pressure mounting in between. But in the end the great preserve was a reality.

If the Point Reyes Peninsula itself is in safe hands today, the same cannot be said for the landscape that faces it across the long blue aisle of Tomales Bay. That eastern shore, where the biggest feeder creeks come down to the bay, is ranchland, not parkland, and Eastman wants to see it kept that way. Older county plans called for tens of thousands of dwellings on these rolling, windswept hills. This seems unlikely now, but the existing pastoral landscape could give way to lavish rural "estates," a gentrification that locals deplore.

Eastman sees a subtler gentrification taking place in Inverness. Summer cottages are being remodeled into lavish year-round homes, and prices are "out of control. There's no place for people to live that want to start out somewhere, doing dishes at the restaurant or making beds, or mending boats or doing landscaping.

"I want to conserve people, too. We are wasting an awful lot of people."

Amy Meyer

—◇◇◇—

Though she might prefer to put it the other way around, conservationist Amy Meyer has also made her mark as a fine artist. In her San Francisco studio, she does collage, an inspired putting together of disparate things. As a conservationist, she has devoted her life to a great project that is more than a little analogous: the sprawling jigsaw puzzle of a park called the Golden Gate National Recreation Area.

At the core of the recreation area is a collection of former U.S. Army lands within sight of the Golden Gate: the Presidio, Fort Mason, the Marin Headlands, Fort Mason, Fort Miley, and Fort Point. Set aside for harbor defense in the middle 1800s, by the middle 1900s these reservations had lost their military importance. There arose twin temptations: to sell off this valuable real estate, and to put utilitarian government buildings on it. Conservationists, valuing these open spaces, blocked many such efforts. An overriding vision, though, was lacking.

In the spring of 1970, the latest raid was pending. Targeted this time was East Fort Miley, a piece of hilltop near Amy Meyer's home where planted pine and cypress trees half-concealed old bunkers and batteries. It struck the federal General Services Administration as a dandy place for a gigantic archives storage building. At a local Sierra Club meeting Meyer attended, someone asked, "What about the archives?" "There was a silence," she recalls. "I felt sort of obliged

to say something." She volunteered to take the issue on.

Unlike the many activists who rise in defense of a place they know and love, Meyer had barely been aware of East Fort Miley. Having finished the most demanding phase of motherhood, she had simply decided, quite in the abstract, to get involved in a neighborhood concern.

"It didn't take very long for me to realize that I had a tiger by the tail."

Instead of dealing with one small parcel, she soon found herself grappling with the fate of all the government lands at the Golden Gate, and more. A federal study, not yet public knowledge, had already raised the possibility of combining several of the old military sites into a federal park. Meyer's stepping forward marked the beginning of a citizen movement that would seize on the original modest park idea and expand it beyond all recognition.

Her chief mentor in this work was the national Sierra Club leader Edgar Wayburn, who had long worked for coastal parks in Marin County. When they got together, the two saw the possibility of a compound preserve—a collage of protected lands—unmatched in the nation. On the San Francisco shore, it could take in not only the military properties but also some intervening city and state parks to create a unified shoreline recreation area. In Marin, the headlands forts could be the southern anchor of a coastal greenbelt running north to Mount Tamalpais or beyond. Meyer and Wayburn saw this seemingly fantastic vision turned into reality in two and a half years.

Wayburn was the strategist; Congressman Phillip Burton was the political muscle; but Meyer was the organizer. It was a skill somehow unexpected in an artist, but one she had always had. "I don't know exactly where it came from. It is not something you learn in a classroom," Meyer says. "In high school back in New York City, I used to organize people to do all kinds of social events. I never particularly analyzed it, I just know that I know how to do it."

As Meyer and Wayburn gathered allies and worked on the project, it seemed to come alive, like a good piece of art, under their hands. The moment was simply right. Far from beating down opposition, park advocates were besieged with offers of support. "Marin was wholeheartedly for it. Anything that doesn't have a house on it, they said, put it in the park. They didn't want Highway One to get bigger; they didn't want this and they didn't want that; and everything they didn't want, we were able to oblige." In the biggest coup of all, Ed Wayburn persuaded Secretary of the Interior Rogers Morton to agree to including within park boundaries the historic ranches of the Olema Valley, thus linking protected lands on Mount Tamalpais with those on Point Reyes.

In 1972, with the backing of the Nixon administration and a happily united Congress, the Golden Gate National Recreation Area came into being. Since then, Meyer has done little else but tend to its health

and continuing expansion—"keeping all the parts together and adding pieces on." The collage has spread a little wider in Marin, picked up a few precious acres in San Francisco, and added significant new pieces in San Mateo County. It now encompasses 75,000 acres, or 115 square miles.

Meyer still co-chairs the organization she founded with Ed Wayburn in 1970, People for a Golden Gate National Recreation Area. She served for almost three decades on a unique Citizens Advisory Commission that helped to guide park policy (until it was discontinued by the Bush administration in 2002). She still sits on the board that governs the historic core of the Presidio, part of the park but with a difference. Faced with the huge expense of maintaining the nation's largest single cluster of historic buildings, Congress has demanded that this section pay its own way through rentals. "And we've got to pay the bills to get the buildings up and running, and we have to fill them with tenants who will contribute to the park."

The Bay Area's people now regard the green lands spreading north and south from the Golden Gate as a birthright, an unquestioned gift from the past. Amy Meyer worries sometimes that this attitude keeps us from attending to the future.

"Some people don't understand, they take it for granted or have no understanding of what it took to keep this the way it is. They think it just somehow came, with the wind! With the waves!

"It doesn't work that way, folks. If you want to keep it, you've got to work for it."

Amy Meyer at Boutelle Battery in the Golden Gate National Recreation Area in San Francisco, 1999

Martin Griffin

—ɯ—

When Martin Griffin was growing up in Utah, his parents had a mountain cabin on the banks of the Ogden River. He has a memory from age three of smells and sounds: the scent of sage, willows, and trout, the noise of the river over which floated, almost too idyllically, the music of his father's mandolin.

During the Depression, the family moved around the West, living in Portland and Los Angeles and finally in Oakland. Griffin remembers Southern California as "still a beautiful Mediterranean paradise." Oakland, though, disappointed him, especially its industrial, inaccessible, and polluted shoreline. The landscape that struck his fancy in the region was Marin County, still lightly peopled.

So it was in Marin County that Griffin, after finishing medical school at Stanford, set up his practice.

Among his first patients was Elizabeth Terwilliger, a birder and activist, who in 1958 recruited him for the board of the new Marin chapter of the Audubon Society and into its first fight, to stop a major marina project on tidal bird habitat in Richardson Bay. At the head of the effort was Caroline Livermore, matriarch of a wealthy Marin family deeply involved in conservation. Griffin helped, watched, and learned as Livermore persuaded the county and the city of Tiburon to buy

and preserve the land at stake. It was the first piece of the San Francisco Bay system ever to be set aside as a biological reserve.

In 1961 Griffin, now president of Marin Audubon, heard about the plans to turn Highway One, the winding coast highway, into a freeway. Griffin set out on a twenty-year effort to frustrate such projects by buying land in their path.

His attention turned first to Bolinas Lagoon, a relatively small but vital estuary at the western foot of Mount Tamalpais. The freeway would traverse its shore, and the lagoon itself was to be dredged and filled for a marina development. Learning that a ranch in the area was about to be subdivided, Griffin approached the owner. The parcel in question was a special one. Not only did it lie athwart the freeway route, but it also contained a "heronry," a grove of redwood trees where herons, egrets, and other water birds roosted and nested. Once common around the Bay Area, such sites had grown rare and precious since World War II.

Taking a green gamble, Griffin put up $1,000 of his own money for an option. "And I persuaded the Marin Audubon Society to buy the ranch for $337,000," he says. "They'd never spent more than $100 to send a ranger to Audubon summer camp!

Martin Griffin at Wohler Bridge on the Russian River, 1998

"We had nine months to raise $90,000, and ten years to raise the balance, at 6 percent interest. That's a lot of money, in those days."

Griffin joined forces with the local Audubon treasurer, Stan Picher, to enlist several Audubon chapters in a statewide campaign on behalf of the place now called Audubon Canyon Ranch. The doctor enlisted his patients, too. "I hit them up for donations! It was a standing joke in the Ross Valley Clinic, where I practiced—don't go see Dr. Griffin unless you want to help buy Audubon Canyon Ranch."

The trees where the big birds nested were safe for the moment, but the mudflats and shallows where they fed in the adjacent lagoon were not. By 1966 the marina plans were rapidly taking shape. The complex would be centered on Kent Island, a dry spot in mid-lagoon, privately owned.

History repeated itself as Griffin approached the owner of the strategic parcel, Anne Kent. "I was flabbergasted that she gave me this option. Then I had a hard time persuading the board of directors of Audubon Canyon Ranch to take it on as a project." He turned to Huey Johnson of The Nature Conservancy, who was able to advance some funds. As a result, the entire lagoon eventually became a wildlife sanctuary.

Throughout the 1970s, Audubon Canyon Ranch continued its acquisitions. It bought more land on Bolinas Lagoon and also picked up other strategic parcels to the north, including important habitats along Tomales Bay and lands that buffered the new

Point Reyes National Seashore. Meanwhile educational programs at the ranch were helping to tip the balance of opinion about development. By 1972, the county had resolved to keep its coastal regions rural, and the state had given up its plans to build the coastal freeway.

In the 1990s, Marin Audubon launched another campaign to influence policy by buying land. Seeking better protection for the shores of San Francisco Bay, the chapter repeatedly stuck its neck out in the fashion pioneered by Marty Griffin. The doctor himself, though, had moved on to other challenges.

In 1975, he had moved north to the banks of the Russian River in Sonoma County near Healdsburg, refurbishing a historic farm as the Hop Kiln Winery. If he had retirement in mind, "I couldn't have picked a more contentious place to buy a ranch than right here." Ravaged by gravel mining in the riverbed, pollution and deforestation in the watershed, and the effects of water diversion, the Russian is in very poor shape. Griffin has thrown himself into the fight to do something about it on a large scale, and in his own backyard.

In cooperation with a neighboring owner, he has worked for years to restore a tributary creek on his property. In 1996, spawning steelhead returned to his stream. As Griffin writes in his book *Saving the Marin-Sonoma Coast*: "Seeing these fish return after thirty years reminded me of the exaltation I felt when we knew we had rescued the great American egrets on Bolinas Lagoon so many years ago."

Kay Holbrook

—⁓—

Some environmentalists seem to draw their strength from a single locale, becoming almost an embodiment of their chosen places. So it is with Kay Holbrook of Inverness on the shore of Tomales Bay in western Marin County.

Inverness is a small town, a green one, a steep one. It occupies a moist hillside on the Point Reyes Peninsula, running down from Inverness Ridge to the silty shore of the long, narrow bay that fills the rift zone of the San Andreas Fault. Since its founding in 1889, Inverness has been a place of second homes and retirement homes, a place to relax for a day or a decade.

Kay Holbrook's grandmother, a San Joaquin Valley resident, bought her Inverness house in 1910 "to get away from the heat." Kay's parents settled in Southern California but kept the place in Inverness. So when Holbrook came north to the University of California at Berkeley in 1929, in a sense she was on home turf. Though Depression financial troubles forced her to drop out in 1931, she stayed in the Bay Area. "All the fun was in Berkeley!" she says. In 1935 she married Brad Holbrook, whose family likewise had an Inverness cottage. The couple lived in Berkeley but was often on the car ferry to Marin.

Kay's own concerns at that time were urban—the Alameda County League of Women Voters, the needs of abandoned children. Gradually, though, her focus shifted. "We were both realizing at that time what was happening in California. And we were particularly protective of Marin County. So I started coming over here for meetings, too."

In 1958, the story broke that the federal government wanted to buy most of the Point Reyes Peninsula for a park. The plan was very controversial, but the Inverness-Berkeley axis was all for it. "An awful lot of us worked awfully hard for that," Holbrook notes.

The work continued even after Point Reyes National Seashore was established in 1962. Congress had appropriated far too little money to buy the Point Reyes ranches, and it took a second mobilization of public opinion to shake loose the funds that made the park complete.

A more local issue that has taken a lot of Holbrook's time is Chicken Ranch Beach, a swimming cove in the heart of Inverness and a town tradition. "I took my children there when they were just babies, when we didn't have any gas during the war and couldn't get out to the other beaches." However, the beach, the bordering water, and the adjacent upland were privately owned. "The owner had quite elaborate development plans for it," Holbrook says. "And he tried to block off public access. So I headed up a committee."

That understates the matter, for the issue consumed tremendous energy, divided the entire town, and ended up in court. In 1972, the California Supreme Court used the Chicken Ranch Beach case to set

important legal doctrine. The justices' decision in *Marks v. Whitney* established once and for all that ownership of tidelands does not bring with it any automatic right to develop them. Remaining issues at Chicken Ranch kept Holbrook busy for years.

In 1974, the Holbrooks settled for good in Inverness. Kay has since been a voice in every environmental issue affecting western Marin County: the expansion and management of parks, the preservation of farmland, the protection of Tomales Bay. But her focus remains her hometown.

"We've had battles trying to maintain the status quo in a way, insofar as keeping our roads fairly narrow," Holbrook says. "We've tried to enforce the county's restrictions about buildings, which in most cases are sensible. We have had disputes about water, whether we should get our water from the North Marin Water Company, or whether we should live with our own resources." Local self-reliance, which Holbrook favored, prevailed. "Almost anything in Inverness can start arguments because we are a small community, you see."

Protective though she is of her home landscape, Holbrook differs sometimes with newer residents who are still less tolerant of change. "Quite a number of people who have come here within the last ten or twelve years have a tremendous interest in the community. They think they discovered paradise. They are afraid of any changes at all." She has parted company with some of her neighbors by supporting the building of affordable housing in Point Reyes Station, four miles from Inverness and the only local town with any room to grow.

"I didn't take as strong a stand as I wish now I had on some things," Holbrook says, "because I hated to offend old friends. Now of course I am so old I don't give a darn."

Does Kay Holbrook have any advice for the young? "I wouldn't have the nerve to give them any advice. I wouldn't think of it. No."

Kay Holbrook at Chicken Ranch Beach in Inverness, 1998

Ellen and Bill Straus

—⁂—

When Ellen Prins told her New York friends that she was going west to marry a California dairyman, "they found it very strange. That was in 1950, and just at that time there was a big movement from the farm to the city. Everything was convenience. It was the beginning of frozen food, all that kind of thing . . . They thought that farms were all very backward."

"But this farm," she adds proudly, "was never backward."

"This farm," the Straus organic dairy on the east shore of Tomales Bay, is now a local fixture, an icon of environmentally sensitive agriculture, and very nearly an object of pilgrimage. But it and its owners have been through some changes.

William Straus grew up in Hamburg, Germany, the son of intellectual Jewish parents. In 1934, twenty years old, he left the deepening shadows of the Third Reich. His travels took him at last to San Francisco. "I had inherited some money," he remembers. "I wanted to live near civilization—not too near, but not too far away." In 1941, he bought a dairy ranch on the east shore of Tomales Bay: a lush slope leaning back from the water, an irregular century-old house among cypress trees. Bill remembers a time when he would go to a concert in San Francisco, get back to Marshall at

1:00 AM, and stay awake to milk the herd two hours later. "Of course, that time has passed."

In 1949, on a trip to New York City, he was introduced to Ellen, a fellow refugee who had fled her native Amsterdam in 1940. When Bill showed her his pictures of the West Marin ranch, she was enchanted. "I told him to put the photographs away. I asked myself, 'Am I going to marry this man just because he has this beautiful farm near the sea?'" Sixteen days later, they were engaged.

From the beginning the Strauses were outsiders. Their accent was different. Their name was different (most Marin ranching families have Italian or Portuguese surnames). Their politics were different (Ellen served several years on the Marin Democratic Central Committee). And they had a different attitude toward their land. Most ranchers accepted, even counted on, the seemingly inevitable urbanization of West Marin; the Strauses were alone in believing—against all evidence—that it might be forestalled. Becoming active conservationists, they did what they could to fend off development. In the early 1970s, when the county changed its policies and determined to keep its coastal regions rural, the Strauses were in there pitching. At one key hearing, they saw the

Ellen and Bill Straus at home in Marshall on Tomales Bay, 1998

hearing room empty as their angry ranching colleagues walked out to protest their stand.

Yet the Strauses are farmers to the core, with exactly the same concerns as their neighbors on the land: the weather, milk prices, the squeeze of rising expenses and limited returns. Thus they are uniquely suited to serve as two-way ambassadors. They can interpret agricultural reality to urbanites and urban environmental concerns to rural dwellers. Largely as a result of their patient presence, the hard feelings between city and country gave way, in the course of the 1970s, to a détente, a friendship even.

Ellen Straus worried that new zoning rules alone would not do the job of keeping farmland open. In 1978, a subdivision near the rural hamlet of Nicasio proved her point. It alarmed environmentalists—and (so greatly had attitudes changed) it worried the farm community as well.

"We need something more permanent," Ellen kept saying. Together with her friend Phyllis Faber, she originated the idea of a Marin Agricultural Land Trust: a private nonprofit corporation, not part of government, focused on farmland specifically, rather than on land in general, and run in large part by the ranchers themselves. This formula was, at the time, unique. The trust set up shop in 1980. Aided by grant money, bond money, and citizen contributions, it has since protected some thirty-six thousand acres in the rolling hills of West Marin.

In 1993, the Straus family began a new venture. Oldest son Albert took the dairy "organic," raising fodder and producing milk without pesticides, herbicides, chemical fertilizers, antibiotics, or hormones. The whole farm has become a demonstration project in sustainable agriculture. Instead of vanishing into the regional milk pool, Straus milk is separately bottled, in their own creamery, in glass, and distributed to a large and loyal clientele in Northern California and beyond.

The Straus experiment exemplifies a trend that many environmentalists welcome. You might call it the de-commodification of food. Most of what we eat and drink hardly betrays its origin; it might have been synthesized in a factory behind the supermarket. If you drink Straus milk, by contrast, you know its history and can point out to your kids the farm it comes from. Such products have a small but growing place in the food supply. To give themselves an edge against larger competitors, Marin county farmers, including the Strauses, have developed their own "Marin Organic" label, allowing the consumer to choose products grown in a specific place as well as according to specific rules.

Phyllis Faber

—m—

If you are passionate enough," says Phyllis Faber of Mill Valley, "you learn a lot." But for Faber, a biologist, it seems to be the learning that comes first, that feeds the springs of the environmental passion.

Raised in New York in the 1930s, Faber studied microbiology at Mount Holyoke and Yale, but it wasn't in those halls that she learned about environmental problems. That message reached her at the Thomas School, a Connecticut prep school where she took a post in 1969. There she met Joy Lee, a pioneering wetlands advocate, and learned of the ecological functions of swamps and marshes. Connecticut's state legislature was considering wetlands protection at the time, and Faber quickly signed up for the cause.

Fortunately for California, if not for Connecticut, there was an abrupt change of plans. Faber's husband's marketing job took him and the family west to Marin County that fall. Faber found that the issues that were simmering in New England were mounting to a boil in her adopted home. Within weeks she was working in the campaign to pass a law to protect the Pacific coastline, including its few remnant wetlands, from overdevelopment. Success came in 1972 when the voters, bypassing a deadlocked legislature, enacted by initiative the California Coastal Zone Conservation Act. Faber was appointed to the North Central Coastal Commission, one of the six regional coastal planning commissions set up under this law.

As a coastal commissioner, Faber found herself seeing with new eyes a world she had known only as a visitor: the rural western part of her new home county, where dairy farms and livestock ranches blanketed most of the land. Tramping those hills on commission business, Faber came to know and admire the men and women who worked so hard there. She tried to make sure that necessary environmental regulation did not degenerate into petty harassment. "The ranchers soon realized that we would never stand in the way of putting up a barn, things like that."

The Marin County board of supervisors had recently decided to preserve rural landscapes but was wondering how to accomplish this goal. Would zoning and regulation do the job? Or could the land somehow be brought into public ownership, as Point Reyes had been, with farmers staying on as government leaseholders?

Faber disliked this second solution. As a commissioner, she had visited properties run by their owners and properties occupied by tenants. She knew which farms looked happier. "It's inescapable," she says. "Land managed by the owner is better off." Yet she also saw clearly that government fiat could not be counted on to fend off subdivision and development forever. Was there a third way?

Faber's companion in these worries was Ellen Straus, the rancher-conservationist from Marshall on

Tomales Bay. One day in 1978, walking side by side through a green pasture, the two women committed themselves to building that third way. The result, several years later, was the Marin Agricultural Land Trust. Faber credits Straus with the idea; Straus credits Faber with the energy to say, "Let's do it." The two served together for years on the trust's rancher-dominated board.

"I think the '70s and '80s were wondrous moments of time in California's history," says Faber. "So much awareness grew, and the system was open to change."

While all this was going on, Faber somehow managed to pursue her scientific and educational work. In 1972, she had helped found the Environmental Forum of Marin, a sort of floating college focusing on local natural history, environmental issues, and planning questions. A *Who's Who* of Marin County would be rich in Forum graduates.

In the same period, she worked on a pioneering attempt to restore a lost wetland: the Muzzi Marsh in Corte Madera. To make up for the damage caused by a new ferry terminal nearby, the old dikes that had turned this plot into dry land were to be breached, readmitting the tide. Would marsh vegetation reappear by itself, or would expensive planting be required? The answer—that cordgrass and pickleweed needed no help to sprout, once the environment had been made right—was the first of many lessons to be learned from the site. Faber now lends her expertise to the far larger wetland restoration projects that are taking shape on the shores of San Francisco Bay.

In 1984, she became the editor of *Fremontia*, the journal of the California Native Plant Society, and spent sixteen years building it into an influential voice. She also took the society into the field of book publishing. And she has had a hand, as writer, editor, or publisher, in most of the recent books in the field of California botany. Her *California's Wild Gardens* is perhaps the definitive popular work in the field. She is a general editor of the natural history series at the University of California Press.

Phyllis Faber at Muzzi Marsh in Corte Madera, 1998

Bill Kortum

When Bill Kortum was growing up in the 1930s in Petaluma, the Sonoma County countryside and coast were his for the exploring. "As kids we could hike and ride where we wanted," he says, "and nobody would bother us. You felt you could go anywhere in the landscape, it belonged to you."

"And I remember my father talking to me about how I'd lose that freedom in my lifetime."

Bill Kortum has devoted much of that lifetime to ensuring that his father's words do not entirely come true.

As a boy, Kortum tended chickens as a chore and cows as a hobby, building a barn as a high school shop project. He went on to a successful veterinary practice. In 1956, after military service, he set up shop in the small, historic settlement of Cotati, midway between Petaluma and Santa Rosa. He became quite a booster, heading the Chamber of Commerce and working to draw a new state college campus, now Sonoma State University, to the area; he initiated the incorporation of the city of Cotati.

Increasingly, though, Kortum became concerned about what he called the "Sonoma Land Rush." Outright urbanization concerned him less than the progressive splitting up of farms, the proliferation of "ranchettes."

In 1965, Kortum's attention was drawn to a coastal property, rich in tide pools, called Salt Point. A federal study had flagged it as a possible park, but no money was in prospect. Kortum, who was serving on a school board at the time, saw how valuable the site could be for outdoor education. He mobilized his colleagues in the schools, found an alternative Sacramento door to knock on, and got the funding for today's Salt Point State Park.

Victory was sweet, but history owes more to the bitter loss that followed. North of Salt Point, plans were afoot for Sea Ranch, an exclusive resort community on a hitherto unheard of scale—a development that would bar the public from the ten miles of shore it spanned. Kortum's memories of childhood freedom came rushing up. "Those tidelands should all be available, every bit of them, for public use!" But the county supervisors approved the Sea Ranch application. The resulting development, though admired for its design, set a dismaying precedent. Was this the future of the California coast?

Sea Ranch was one of several "last straws" that led citizens to work for a new way of regulating coastal development, the Coastal Commission system. Kortum was in on the fight from the start and chaired the

Bill Kortum near the hiking trail named in his honor at Sonoma Coast State Beach, 2004

statewide advocacy group, the California Coastal Alliance.

After the Coastal Initiative passed in 1972, Kortum hoped to be appointed to one of the regional commissions set up by the law. That he was passed over still rankles a bit. But the effect was simply to turn his attention inland, where the "Sonoma Land Rush" was now in full swing.

Kortum saw the key to preserving the Sonoma County he loved in preserving its agriculture; and he saw the key to preserving agriculture in a novel synergy: the use of treated urban wastewater to irrigate farmers' fields. In 1973, Kortum approached the county, the city of Rohnert Park, and the local Farm Bureau to propose a pilot wastewater irrigation project. It was a success. Within a few years, over eight thousand acres were in production. Regional conservation leader Dorothy Erskine dubbed it the Triple Use Plan: the same acreage serving to grow high-value crops, harmlessly absorb wastewater, and preserve the rural landscape.

Santa Rosa, by far the largest city in the county, was meanwhile wrestling with its own wastewater problem. Its treated sewage was no longer welcome on the traditional dumping ground, the Russian River. If all that wastewater went into "triple use," a vast farm greenbelt would be preserved.

In the end, however, the city took another course and went with a plan to pump most of the water three thousand feet up into the Mayacamas Mountains and inject it into the underground steam field at The Geysers, where it would serve to generate geothermal power. "For Santa Rosa to take that much water and give it to the energy industry is a real insult to this agricultural county," Kortum contends.

Bill Kortum also spent two years on the Sonoma County board of supervisors, pushing for completion of a county general plan, and joined like-minded colleagues in imposing a temporary ban on lot splits. That brought the opposition out in force, and he lost his job in a recall election.

Nevertheless, the ship of land use policy continued its slow change of course. In 1990, the voters established a countywide open space district supported by a quarter-cent sales tax. Fifty thousand acres have now been preserved by this body and the Sonoma Land Trust, a parallel private organization. And voters in eight Sonoma County cities have taken growth control into their own hands, legislating urban growth boundaries to contain development. Bill Kortum has been a steady presence in all of these campaigns.

On the family ranch in Penngrove, where he lives with his wife, Lucy, he can look out the window at the barn he built as a boy. It still solidly stands.

So do the planning and preservation structures that Bill Kortum helped to build for his home county—and for the entire state.

Ledyard Stebbins

If you ask the botanist Ledyard Stebbins, founder of the California Native Plant Society, whether he is an environmentalist, he answers soberly, "Environmentalists usually don't know much about genes." He has heard the key word in its scientific sense, not its political one. Genes and the environment are the two things that go into making organisms from slime molds to people what they are. Which aspect you choose to emphasize, or simply to study, makes you an environmentalist or a geneticist. He himself is an eminent example of the latter.

Stebbins was born in 1906 and grew up in New York and New England; his father owned property in Maine. "I loved to go on long walks from Seal Harbor to various areas in what became Acadia National Park," he says. "I decided to learn the names of all of the flowering plants, trees, and shrubs on Mt. Desert Island and the places where they grew. In two years I knew just about everything, and I had come across species that hadn't previously been known on the island."

Pursuing this new interest at Harvard, he began to wonder if a botanist could make a living. He turned for advice to his businessman father, who seems to have been a good friend to his oddball son. "So he went to campus, and talked with various professors, and ended up by saying that you will never be rich but you can make a life, and I can help you in the early years."

Stebbins's academic career unfolded at Harvard, Colgate, and the University of California at Berkeley. In California, he studied the native grasses of the hills, largely displaced by exotic species from the Mediterranean but hanging on here and there. He wanted to find out if these natives could be modified to better support grazing by cattle and sheep. "I brought in from the wild various grasses that I thought could be improved and grew them in the garden," he says. To his disappointment he found that indigenous plants could not be adapted to the brutal California combination of grazing and summer drought. The Mediterranean imports had flourished for a reason. "I nevertheless explored the genetics of various groups of grasses."

That work led in 1950 to the book *Variation and Evolution in Plants,* which became a landmark in the field. "Professors teaching evolution were much more successful if they wrote about nice cuddly mice or beautiful flapping butterflies, rather than ordinary grasses," Stebbins says with some acerbity. "Nevertheless, that book cemented my reputation." He was elected to the National Academy of Sciences in 1952, the first in a long list of honors.

Also in 1950, Stebbins was asked to head up the Department of Genetics at the newly founded University of California at Davis. He is credited with helping not just that department, but also the entire new campus, get off to a strong start.

"Ledyard looks at everything with questions," his friend and colleague Phyllis Faber says. "There isn't

anything he sees that he takes for granted. He'll look at a pine tree that has two different sizes of cones and he'll conjecture what the evolutionary reason might be. Any differences that he sees in a population of plants, he'll be noticing in terms of evolutionary significance."

"What is the relative importance," Stebbins asks, "of knowing about the environment in which animals and plants and microorganisms are evolving as compared to knowing about the genes that are doing the evolving? I believe they are equally important and complementary to each other. I think that the younger students don't understand how changes in the environment can very subtly support new combinations of genes and bring about evolution."

Stebbins's conservation career, strictly speaking, began as his academic retirement approached. In 1965, he joined a small group of "dedicated seniors" at U.C. Berkeley to prevent the threatened dismantling of a native plant garden in Tilden Park. The group developed into the California Native Plant Society, which

Stebbins describes as "a small but effective unit in a worldwide federation of societies dedicated to saving the beauties of plant life from extinction."

From 1966 to 1982, Stebbins served as president as the organization spread statewide. In 1988, he set up a watch list of endangered plant varieties, which the society maintains to this day. One of many key sites the society has helped to preserve is Ring Mountain in Marin County, where the strange rock called serpentine supports rarities including the Tiburon mariposa lily, *Calochortus tiburonensis.*

"Ledyard doesn't get upset unless there is some scientific basis," Phyllis Faber notes. In the 1960s, when First Lady Ladybird Johnson was urging people to scatter wildflower seeds at random, many botanists worried the wrong plants would get established in the wrong places. Stebbins didn't join in this particular alarm. "They'll die if they're supposed to," he said.

Many things also are dying that are not supposed to, and for these Ledyard Stebbins has been a scrupulous, powerful voice.

Ledyard Stebbins in his garden in Davis, 1998

Luna Leopold

In 1949, Luna Leopold interrupted his scientific career to do a stint of editorial work. At hand was a brilliant but uneven manuscript, the work of his just-deceased father Aldo, called "Great Possessions." What emerged from the process was one of the most-read and best-loved environmental works of the twentieth century, *A Sand County Almanac.*

This is not a story he tells much, for Luna Leopold, placed by the American Geological Institute "among the most distinguished earth scientists of the last half century," has no need to lean on his father's reputation. He studied engineering at the University of Wisconsin, spent World War II with the Army Weather Service, and in 1950 went to work for the United States Geological Survey in Washington, D.C. It was his ambition from the start to quantify things: to characterize in concrete, numerical terms earth processes that until then had been only impressionistically described.

As time went on, Leopold made a specialty of that fascinating, powerful, mercurial, yet ultimately predictable creature, the free-flowing river. He showed, for instance, that a stream's meanders tend to assume a geometrical form in which each pair of bends, each S-shaped curve, is about ten times as long as the width of the stream when it is brimming with water.

During the Kennedy, Johnson, and Nixon administrations, Leopold became a de facto conservation advisor to several successive secretaries of the interior. He recalls the day that Stewart Udall asked his opinion about dams in the Grand Canyon. "He said, 'Luna, you've been down the Grand Canyon. Is it worth saving?' And I said, 'Mr. Secretary, if you want to be the greatest interior secretary that ever lived, you go against the dams in the Grand Canyon, and you'll make a reputation for yourself.' And two weeks later he did so."

Called in again to consult on a huge jetport proposed for the edge of the Everglades, Leopold prepared what amounted to the nation's first environmental impact report. The jetport, he concluded, might not be so bad in itself; but the other development it would attract around it would be deeply harmful to the natural systems of the Everglades. The airport plan was shelved.

Then there was the Alaska oil pipeline. When it was first proposed, Leopold was asked to make a snap assessment of the plan. "Well, they rolled into my office a report that was five feet tall. And I said, 'How much time do I have to review this report?' And they said, 'Fifteen minutes.' I said, 'Very well.' I took the top volume off and opened it up, and I looked at what they

Luna Leopold at home in Kensington, 2002

99

had proposed with regard to the cross-section of the pipeline. And it was a diagram about this large, about two by three inches. It showed a round place, which was the pipe; it showed a bunch of gravel underneath; that was it. No discussion of permafrost, no discussion of river crossings. And I said, 'Very well, I've reviewed it.' And I went up to see my director, and I said, 'You've got to turn this down. This is simply unsatisfactory. They don't know what they're up against.'"

The pipeline that was finally constructed, five years of study and refinement later, was far less damaging than the initial plan would have been. "It's bad enough as it is," says Leopold, "but it would have been awful."

While at the Geological Survey, he also took a stand against the use of motor vehicles to reach weather data stations in wilderness areas. "I objected to using any kind of machines in the wilderness. And I was very highly criticized for that." But he prevailed.

In 1972, Leopold retired from the Survey and moved west to Berkeley, becoming a professor at the University of California. (In this he was following the westward-tending footsteps of his older brother Starker, an eminent wildlife biologist.) In the West, he focused ever more tightly on the nature and problems of streams. Those problems are many, he says. "There are a lot of people harming rivers."

About the most profound change people make in rivers is to dam them and reduce their peak flows. There is much talk today of removing dams, Leopold notes, but he advises against exaggerated hopes: most of these barriers are going to remain. The question then is how to limit, and partially undo, the ecological damage done. Leopold works with younger colleagues who are testing, on the Trinity River and other streams, how "the ruined river below a dam" can be restored to something like health. The big, unregulated stream of pre-dam days is gone, yet a respectable small stream can evolve, with help, so that it supports gravel bars and pools, riparian vegetation and fish, in a diminished version of the natural pattern. "At least we have a set of principles," Leopold says.

In the case of the shrunken river, as in the case of the Alaska pipeline, Leopold's experience seems to contain a lesson: that defeat need not be total. Impacts, however bad, can be reduced. Natural systems can be salvaged in some part. In a world of constant ecological breakage, it is surely good to be reminded that even the fragments are worthy of our care.

Raymond Dasmann

For a generation of Californians, awareness of what human hungers were doing to the natural endowment of the state began with the book *The Destruction of California*, written in 1965 by Raymond Dasmann.

Born in San Francisco in 1919, Dasmann seemed destined to be a ranger, not a writer. Each of two admired older brothers had studied forestry at the University of California, Berkeley and then gone to work for the U.S. Forest Service, one as a timber specialist, the other in range management. Raymond started down the same road, with a detour imposed by World War II. By 1946 he was at Berkeley, newly married, working toward the traditional Dasmann forestry degree.

But Raymond had always had an eye for wildlife—as a youngster he'd taught himself to identify all the birds in Golden Gate Park—and a nagging concern for what was happening to the creatures of the land. At Berkeley, he absorbed the detailed story of habitat loss from teachers like Carl Sauer and Frank Pitelka. When he heard of a novel course in a novel field called wildlife management, taught by A. Starker Leopold, Dasmann switched majors to zoology in order to enroll. He was such a standout in that class that Leopold hired him to do fieldwork on deer populations. So much for forestry; so much for an early departure from the academic world. "I was paid to do the research that gave me my two higher degrees," Dasmann remarks. "That's unusual!"

Dasmann knew too much already to experience some sudden conversion, but the more he studied and the more he observed in the field, the more deeply he became alarmed at the ecological disaster that population growth and reckless exploitation were bringing to the land.

He was teaching at Humboldt State University (then College) in Arcata when he got the chance to write a textbook called *Environmental Conservation*, published in 1959 (and now in its fifth edition). "It was the first attempt, I think, to bring ecology into the conservation textbook area." Most earlier works, he says, "came more from the economic side of things."

The classroom success of the first book brought him the contract to write the more popular *Destruction of California*, a trade book. Many more publications followed. Contrasting himself to activists like his friend Martin Litton, he remarks with self-deprecation: "I tend to operate from the shelter of a classroom. I tend to sit in there and type or scribble."

Dasmann is no optimist. "I think basically we are in denial about this whole thing, the human race is in denial. We don't want to know that things are as bad as they are. We are eroding our own base. It is very difficult to see how we are going to get out of it.

"We have this tremendous environmental movement now, and yet we keep losing ground. With millions of people actively interested in protecting the

environment, we should be able to do enough to actually save a great deal. But we just don't—we're not managing.

"Do I have to end on a hopeful note?"

"The dire headlines of the day are not dire enough."

Yet Dasmann does draw hope, almost in spite of himself, from the ability of people to learn, and to teach. "The greatest thing, I think, is to start telling kids about the world they live on and what it takes to make it function. The dependence of people on the work done by green plants. The fact that ecosystems exist and that you are part of them and you depend on them and you really can't substitute for them. Where does your water come from? Where does your air come from? Where does your food come from? What does it take to produce it? These things should be right there from the early grades on. And yet, I think in most places, you can manage to get a Ph.D. without even asking those questions, let alone answering them.

"We have just got to become aware of where we are living and what it is going to take to enable us to continue. There is no avoiding it."

Dasmann draws hope, too, from his family: his wife, Elizabeth Sheldon, whom he met as a soldier in Australia in 1944, and his three daughters. Like the thinkers known as ecofeminists, he sees women as likelier than men to respond to and care for the land, providing a needed balance to "the heavy masculine side." He adds, "I don't see how we are going to get very far with dealing with the world's problems unless we enlist the half of the human race that historically hasn't been able to play a role in planning for the future and making it happen. I think it is absolutely essential that we do that."

Raymond Dasmann at the Presidio shoreline in San Francisco, 1998

Jean Rusmore
and Frances Spangle

—⁓—

Jean Rusmore and Frances Spangle came from opposite directions to meet in the Peninsula town of Portola Valley, to make their mark as environmentalists, and to create a series of lively hiking guides used by thousands.

Born in 1920, Rusmore grew up in Anaheim "before Disneyland" and spent every summer on the wide-open Southern California beaches. World War II changed the coastline of her childhood forever. "When the Navy took over places that had been resorts and built munitions plants on marshland, I was shocked," she says.

Frances Spangle, member of an old Marin family, grew up in Sausalito before the building of the Golden Gate Bridge. As a child she wandered over the open slopes now slashed by Highway 101. "The place where there is this enormous cut was a wonderful hill, with windblown oak trees and flowers all over; ground iris and lupines, everything. I used to know absolutely every one of them," Spangle says.

War and marriage took both women back east. In the early 1950s the Rusmore and Spangle families arrived in Portola Valley, almost together, and built neighboring houses. The women soon became hiking companions and embarked on parallel conservation careers.

At this time, urban development had just about finished consuming the orchards of the Peninsula and the Santa Clara Valley and was set to begin climbing into the bordering mountains. As is often the case, the rapid growth produced belated opposition, rather as a serious infection summons antibodies forth.

Spangle was one of the organizers of the Peninsula's highly effective Committee for Green Foothills. She describes the committee's work like this: "You find out how it is done; what commission is reviewing whatever it is; the plans and what projects are threatening, raising their ugly heads, and you go ahead and do something about it.

"I remember a hearing in Half Moon Bay, when they were trying to put a freeway across the McNee Ranch, which has some of the most beautiful wildflowers up there in the world. It was a huge meeting, everybody down there, from all sides. Hundreds of people. Well, I spoke my piece." Spangle's description of the values of the land proved important. "When I went out of there, the lawyers followed me out. If something

Jean Rusmore at a Midpeninsula Regional Open Space District preserve in the Santa Cruz Mountains, 1998

gets in the record, it can have an impact. And now, twenty years later, they have really stopped this terrible roadway that was going to be connected."

Jean Rusmore's environmental work started in the late 1960s with the League of Women Voters. Then she spent some time working for the Committee for Green Foothills as a legislative advocate. She found, however, that behind-the-scenes lobbying was not her game. "I found it quite taxing," she recalls. "I like to state the position and give all the appropriate reasons, the common-sense reasons as well as the legal ones, and then I would like to assume that legislators will use their good sense and go that way. I found it very hard to see that they weren't always swayed. So I only did it for three years." She admires the staying power of her successor, Lennie Roberts.

The voters had by this time established a Midpeninsula Regional Open Space District, which was buying land and making it available for recreation. Spangle and Rusmore simultaneously felt the urge to spread the word about these new destinations. Rusmore remembers: "We thought it would be nice to do a book, and that we would probably publish it ourselves." The realities of self-publication proved discouraging, though. "No way were we going to keep all those books in the basements we didn't have!"

So the two women took the draft manuscript of *Peninsula Trails* to Tom Winnett, owner of the prominent guidebook publisher Wilderness Press. Spangle recalls: "We went in on Tuesday, showed him our sheets that were all done on one side of our husbands' used-up stationery. On Saturday he called up and said, 'I will take it.' So we had to scramble and really put it together."

As any guidebook writer will tell you, hiking for research, with mind and pen and camera busy, is quite a different thing from hiking for fun. "If we walked six or eight or nine miles in one day, that would be the most," Spangle says. "We found we couldn't get all our friends to go with us; you have to spend too much time talking at them."

In their write-ups, Spangle and Rusmore never settled for giving dry directions and mileages. "We talked about the geology and the climate and heaven knows what," Spangle says. "We gave some of the history. We put it all together."

Peninsula Trails appeared in 1982 and vastly exceeded its authors'—and publisher's—hopes. Spangle remembers the call she got from Tom Winnett: "I don't know why I was surprised, Frances, but somebody came in from Western Books and said 'I'd like five hundred copies.' And I said, 'Oh, we'll get them out as soon as we can.' And he said, 'I want them right now!'" Spangle and Rusmore's second and more ambitious book, *South Bay Trails*, was equally successful. Both have been through several revisions and are still in print. Rusmore has done a third book, *The Bay Area Ridge Trail: Ridgetop Adventures above San Francisco Bay*.

"We hope that those who come to know these places will appreciate them and become stewards of the lands," Rusmore says.

Both women are still on the trail. Every month Rusmore takes a group known as the Walkie-Talkies on a hike, imparting her knowledge of the country. Spangle is leading groups outdoors and sharing her experiences with armchair hikers at the retirement home where she now lives. "I write out something each time and give it to everybody. People here say, 'I can't go on those walks, but I like to read about them!'"

Frances Spangle at Rodeo Beach in the Marin Headlands, 1998

Harold Gilliam

—ɷ—

Growing up in Hollywood during the Depression, Harold Gilliam knew the Hollywood Hills when they were partly wild. In Nichols Canyon, he discovered a thirty-foot waterfall: "the thrill of my young life." As bulldozers and steam shovels moved in to mine the hills for gravel and prepare them for development, he and his young friends fantasized sabotage. He would develop more effective tools.

Gilliam studied political science and economics at UCLA and then at U.C. Berkeley, with a long break for World War II. After the war, he went through the Stanford Writing Program, headed by Wallace Stegner, and subsequently got a job at the *San Francisco Chronicle*. Following tradition at that time, he began at the bottom—"I went from being an officer in the Army to being a copy boy"—but soon was writing news digests and occasional articles for the Sunday supplement "This World."

In 1953, a piece on San Francisco Bay brought Gilliam an offer from Doubleday to do a book. *San Francisco Bay* appeared in 1957. Though not environmental in focus, it raised an early alarm about the filling of the Bay. Three more books followed in rapid succession, including the influential *Island in Time*, an eloquent plea for the preservation of Point

Reyes. David Brower put a copy of that on every desk in Congress.

In 1960, Gilliam resumed his newspaper career, launching the weekly column called "This Land." It appeared briefly in the *San Francisco Examiner* and then in the *Chronicle* for more than thirty years. It made him both a keen observer and a significant shaper of the local environmental scene.

In 1964, as the San Francisco Freeway Revolt neared its climax, Gilliam toured the state to report on the effects of such freeways elsewhere. Editor Scott Newhall ran the resulting pieces on the front page. "I compared the Division of Highways to the Southern Pacific Railroad in the old days, as in Frank Norris's novel, *The Octopus*." Shortly after that the *Chronicle* held an anti-freeway rally in Golden Gate Park. Gilliam remembers with amusement how the papers covered the rally: the *Chronicle*'s photographer shot close-ups of a crowd, while the *Examiner* photographed the gathering from the air, making it look insignificantly small.

At a time when nuclear power was regarded as benign, Gilliam was one of the first writers anywhere to look into its drawbacks (to the displeasure of the *Chronicle* owners, who, however, gave him his head).

Harold Gilliam near Baker Beach in the Golden Gate National Recreation Area in San Francisco, 2004

He gave serious ink to the possibility of bringing back ferries at a time when that seemed a quaint anachronism. "Why not bring back the horse and buggy?" a *Chronicle* colleague mocked. But a ferry system is in place and expanding today.

Gilliam helped to open the uncomfortable subject of seismic hazard in the Bay Area. "At that time you didn't talk about things like this. So when there was an earthquake that did some damage out in the west part of the city here, I did some stories on the constant danger and what we're doing about it or not doing about it. Since then it's been fairly common knowledge."

The list goes on and on.

During his first decade as a columnist, Gilliam somehow squeezed in a Washington career. He served as an editorial assistant to Interior Secretary Stewart Udall and helped in the preparation of Udall's 1963 book on the environment, *The Quiet Crisis*. He also served on several high-level advisory boards and worked quietly on the federal end to help local activists head off a proposed bridge from San Francisco to Marin via Angel Island and an atomic power plant on Bodega Head.

Gilliam remembers the first meeting of what would become the Save San Francisco Bay Association, to which he was invited as an observer. He went, listened, approved, and departed feeling that there was very little hope. He watched in astonishment and delight as the movement took off, overcame what seemed insurmountable obstacles, and reached its goal of halting bay fill. Gilliam's own 1969 book, *Between the Devil and the Deep Blue Bay*, helped make the case for the permanent Bay Conservation and Development Commission.

Since then, he says, he has seen this kind of miracle repeated many times. "The moral is, if you're going to do something, you've got to start at the bottom, and not expect that somebody at the top is going to do it." This is perhaps the greatest lesson he draws from half a century on the environmental beat: "People power works."

Gilliam is deeply concerned about growth in California and is more willing than most to talk about immigration, an issue that pulls him both ways, just as it divides the environmental community. "There are now more than ten times as many people in California as there were when I was growing up. Are there going to be ten times again as many? You talk about the population leveling off at a certain point, but that's global. People will keep coming in to California as long as they can. And I feel deeply for the people who struggle to get across the border, at great cost to themselves.

"But at the same time we should be asking, Is there enough water for those numbers of people? Are we going to use salt water? If so, how much is it going to cost? What are the waste products? Are we going to pave over the Central Valley, get rid of agriculture? So what do we eat and where is it going to come from and how much is it going to cost to import it?

"Somebody's got to look into all of this. There should be some kind of a high-level foundation to study the future of California with unlimited population increase."

When it comes to putting his finger on big problems, Harold Gilliam hasn't lost the knack.

Cecelia Hurwich

—⁓—

Cecelia Hurwich, feminist, environmentalist, and peace activist, makes a habit of fresh starts. After earning a degree in psychology from the University of California at Berkeley in 1941, she volunteered for navy service as a WAVE. She met her husband, Rudy Hurwich, in the military and raised a family in Berkeley. When her three children had started school, Hurwich returned to school herself, studying design at the California College of Arts and Crafts. During what is usually called the prime of life, interior design was her career. But her real calling seems to have come to her as she was approaching age sixty, when her beloved mother died.

"I realized," says Hurwich, "that I didn't have a single friend over seventy who was part of my life. I said, who am I going to learn from about aging now?" She felt a powerful need to get to know older women at their best. Again she went back to school, casting her quest in the form of a master's thesis. She found that most research on aging focused on the negative aspects only—aging as decline—and that it focused on men. "I put out a call to the community, that I wanted women who had a zest for living, who were enjoying later life, and who seemed to be doing something meaningful."

The master's turned into a doctorate, and by the time she received that degree, in 1990, Hurwich herself had reached the seventy mark. She had also become a sought-after expert on the art of aging, female division. Now she lectures and presents seminars to women all over the world. "As older women," she says, "we are a considerable force once we own our own strength. We can use it by becoming teachers, knowing who we are and that we have something to say."

Two other threads come in. One is activism against war. World War II, though a just one in her view, left her with horrifying memories. "I took that whole experience—all of us did—and just pushed it under the table." Later she became determined to do whatever she could to fend off war and preparations for war.

The second thread is the environment. "I became an environmentalist in college," she says, "when I worked in Yosemite during summer vacations. I met students there from all over the world. Some friends had motorcycles, and we would go motorcycling to a trailhead or even zoom up to Tuolumne Meadows for a hike." She also saw people abusing the park—feeding the bears, dumping trash in the river, lighting smoky fires—and felt the first stirrings of concern. "People weren't educated," she recalls. "They didn't know.

"The thing I got from Yosemite," Hurwich says, "was my connection to the natural world." This imprint has led her to contribute to the Yosemite Fund, a partnership that underwrites needed improvements and restorations in the park. "It gives me the satisfaction of knowing our efforts to help preserve the park will benefit future generations."

Now she mingles her causes, green and gray. "I believe that you can't have a vital life unless you have a healthy planet. One of the things I am most interested in now is endocrine disruptors and POPs—persistent organic pollutants. Those chemicals are in the air and affect everybody's health."

Recently she helped found a group called Earth Elders. "We live sustainably; we teach others to live sustainably. We work within groups, we work individually. We try to act as role models through our own living. We try to avoid this over-consumerism."

In a lighter vein, Hurwich and other women are showing the way through the group called Great Old Broads for Wilderness, founded in 1989 by Susan Tixier. The "GOBs" began when one of the agencies in charge of the public lands, the federal Bureau of Land Management, proposed to build roads into a scenic and hitherto wild area in Colorado. One of the agency's rationales was, as Hurwich puts it, "that old people have to be able to drive in. Otherwise they can't see how beautiful it is." Only one group could credibly rebut such an argument. "So Susan and a group of about twenty older women put on their backpacks and walked into this area, and got the newspapers and TV and big media to show up, and this was her answer. She said, 'We can backpack in here! We don't need cars.' The road was never built.

"So each year now we choose an area to defend and have what's called a Broad Walk. We walk for a week or a month in this area." One place the Broads have visited is Grand Staircase–Escalante National Monument in Utah. "Conoco has had leases to drill for oil there, and twice in two years we have made such a fuss, and gotten such tremendous reaction, that Conoco has dropped their oil lease on this exquisite national monument."

Hurwich is one who welcomes questions about spiritual stirrings in the wilderness. "I had some out-of-body experiences, where I felt I wasn't here, that I was out there someplace, in heaven, or on the top of a peak. Not dreams, but living dreams, wide-awake visions." One such moment came in the Sierra's Evolution Valley. Arriving in camp early, she felt a sudden urge to go for a jog on a path along the Kings River. "So I started to run. The current happened to be moving in the same direction as I was running. And all of a sudden I felt as if I was lifted and I was flying, just like a bird. It felt as if I was up high, floating with the current."

Cecelia Hurwich at Claremont Canyon Regional Preserve in Berkeley, 1998

Peggy Wayburn

When she came west from Long Island in 1945 to take a job at the San Francisco office of the J. Walter Thompson advertising agency, Peggy Elliott knew who she was. "Being a successful career woman was my ideal," says Wayburn, "and I worked hard at the image, bending over my typewriter with a cigarette handy to inhale. I had a reputation for taking a taxi to cross the street."

Her calculations were upset two years later, when she encountered Edgar Wayburn, a young physician just out of the air force. They met at a party, and he invited her for a hike. She accepted, gladly and innocently, and prepared with a shopping trip. "I went down to the City of Paris, which was then *the* department store, and bought a pair of white shorts and a sleeveless blue shirt, I remember, and a pair of sneakers, and bobby socks, of course."

When the hikers stopped by at Peggy's apartment to pick her up on the appointed morning, she was taken aback. "Here came these three people. They were all dressed in boots and jeans. I remember thinking, My God, who are these rough people!" The group drove up to Pan Toll on the shoulder of Mount Tamalpais, hiked down fifteen hundred feet on the well-named Steep Ravine Trail, and swam in the ocean at Stinson Beach. There remained the return hike. Ed recalls,

"I volunteered to go up and get the car and bring it down. She said, 'You are not, I'm going to walk.' And she walked, and from then on she has walked and walked and walked."

Six months after the blisters had healed, the couple was married. As a wedding present, Peggy gave up smoking.

"Hiking wasn't the only thing I learned from my husband," Peggy Wayburn recalls. "Early on, I was exposed to his grand ideas for a great San Francisco Bay National Park, for preserving earth's beautiful places and for keeping as much of it as wild and untouched as we could. I really didn't understand, but being a good wife, I pretended to."

Then, in the summer of 1948, the Wayburns went on a Sierra Club backpacking trip to the High Sierra. "I can remember the switchbacks," says Peggy. "I can remember going back and forth, back and forth. I can't tell you how miserable I was. God, it was just awful. We finally got to the top, and I collapsed into my sleeping bag. I pulled the hood up, and I was lying there in the dark and looking at the night sky with all the stars and relaxing. There was a rock avalanche I heard, and I remember thinking: that would have happened with no one to hear it. It was just the sound of the wilderness

Peggy Wayburn with her husband, Edgar, on Glacier Bay in Alaska, 1998

to me. The spirit entered into me, and it has been there ever since. I understood what Ed had been talking about, and I became his best and most ardent convert."

Often they operated as a team. Daughter Cynthia recalls their parallel ways of working a room: "My dad was right, but it was my mother who got the Yes." It was Peggy Wayburn who told Stewart Udall, President Kennedy's secretary of the interior, about the dwindling California redwoods and planted the idea of a federal role in protecting them.

In the ensuing campaign for creation of Redwood National Park, Peggy's old skills came back into use. She wrote copy for the ads the Sierra Club placed in national newspapers; she edited and partly wrote the second edition of the Club's influential book, *The Last Redwoods*. Then she produced her own first book, an eloquent brief for the value of estuaries titled *The Edge of Life*.

In 1967, the Wayburns planned a northern vacation. Ed favored Canada, but Peggy wanted to see Alaska's Mount McKinley. "We took the train from Fairbanks," says Peggy. "I close my eyes now, and I can see the mountain. I think we both fell in love with

Alaska there." Since then the couple has returned to Alaska some thirty-five times.

That experience propelled Ed Wayburn to leadership in an epochal national campaign for national parks and protected areas on the arctic frontier. It sent Peggy Wayburn back to the typewriter. The first result was a lavish coffee table book, *Alaska: The Great Land*—instrumental, Ed says, in persuading Congress to pass the Alaska National Interest Lands Conservation Act of 1980. There followed the travel guide *Adventuring in Alaska*. In her research, Peggy says, "I'd try to answer every question I had." Much more than a guidebook, *Adventuring* "starts with the fundamentals of geology and goes on to the biology, and then to people, historically, coming in, and then to the present day. It took me two years to write it."

Adventuring in Alaska is now in its fourth revised edition. Seeing a successful model, the Sierra Club launched a series of "Adventuring" titles in the same style. It includes another Wayburn hit, the local guidebook *Adventuring in the San Francisco Bay Area*.

So Peggy Wayburn must love to write? She gives the writer's answer: "It is awfully hard."

Wim deWit

Before the 1960s, Wim deWit, young father of five, had never taken a vacation. With that many mouths to feed, "you take your vacation money but you keep on working," says deWit. Then he got a job as a tool-maker at Hewlett-Packard in Palo Alto. "They said you have to take a vacation. H-P put me on the road, so to speak."

The road led first to predictable places like Disneyland, but the deWits found themselves wanting something different, something more. "And we learned about a lake in Yosemite, in the high country, that has a walk-in campground. You park the car and tote everything in to the campsite." The toting went well. Then came the first tentative longer hikes, and a day in 1962 that Wim never forgot. "I remember going higher, and there was one area where the water was just running off the rocks, and all you had to do was fall on your belly and drink the water off the land. That was where and when I became an environmentalist!"

One thing kept leading to another. Family hikes became family backpacks. Someone he met on the trail told him about the Sierra Club, and he joined and became active in the Loma Prieta Chapter. "I got all kinds of troubles, nice troubles!" He rang doorbells, served on the chapter governing committee, helped decide pro or con on political endorsements. A job he relished was welcoming new members, making them feel connected and at home. He's done something sim-ilar for Sierra Club leaders from other states, in town for meetings at the national headquarters in San Francisco. Showing guests from Texas, say, around the Bay and up Mount Tamalpais, he's enjoyed the appreciative words, the open mouths.

When his kids were in the Scouts, deWit met the owners of a property called Hidden Villa, backed up to the Santa Cruz Mountains in Los Altos Hills. Here Frank and Josephine Duveneck and their family kept a sort of outdoor open house for visitors, especially little ones. Youngsters came from all over the South Bay to walk its garden and olive grove, to stroke the farm animals in its barnyard, and to hike its forested hillsides—the part deWit calls "the wilder-nice." As a Boy Scout leader and as a parent, he was often there. "When it comes to raising kids," he says, "Mother Nature is the one to help you. And all I had to do was pick up the phone and talk to Mrs. Duveneck, and she said, 'Oh yeah, come on over. You know the rules.'"

In 1985, when deWit retired from Hewlett-Packard, he felt the freedom to do this educational work on a larger scale. He became a docent at Hidden Villa (now run by a nonprofit group) and served a stint on the board of the Midpeninsula Regional Open Space District, where he pushed for ever more environmental education. He laughs at his shock at the title this role brought with it: "The first time I got a letter in the mail addressed to Honorable Wim deWit, I just couldn't believe it! I went to my wife— 'Hey, look at that! Honorable!'"

DeWit takes special pleasure in introducing inner city youngsters to the semi-wilderness of Hidden Villa. "These kids may never have been outside their neighborhoods, so they get a little apprehensive. And I kind of build it up, maybe. I ask them, 'Do you think it is dangerous?' I get both Yes and No. So I explain that it is a much safer place here than when it is dark and you are in the parking lot. And I ask them what the Indians call the wilderness in their language. They call it home! And it was our home, too, a much longer time ago. Then I walk the trails with them, for an hour and a half or two hours. They are curious, and they want to know this, and they want to know that. Kids' questions are easy enough to answer. You don't have to be a biologist. And that is the satisfaction."

One of deWit's favorite memories is the day at Hidden Villa when his class had an unplanned encounter with the facts of life. "We came to the pigpens, and I see that one of the sows is nuzzling up to the boar, but he is asleep! But he eventually gets up, and to make a long story short, they mate, and I am standing there with six or eight little third- or fourthgraders, and I'm just yapping off the top of my head, the most natural thing in the world!"

Though buoyed by his educational work, deWit worries about the future. "First of all, I believe we are ruining this place, this Earth. Our present grandchildren will still live in a viable world. But what about a hundred years from now—what is going to happen? You see it going down.

"Anyway, with children you cannot talk about those things. You have to remain positive. You fight a good fight; you teach them the good things. And from there on, you just hope!"

Wim deWit at Hidden Villa in Los Altos, 1997

Elizabeth Terwilliger

To mainlanders, tropical islands are exotic places. But to people raised on oceanic islands, it is continents, in their hugeness and diversity, that seem wondrous. So it was for Elizabeth Terwilliger, who grew up in the 1910s and 1920s on a sugar cane plantation near Honolulu on Oahu. In 1936 she came to Stanford to study at its school of nursing. California was a revelation—all that freedom of movement, all those varieties of beauty, all that *room*. On her first vacation break, she headed for Yosemite. The memory still thrills her: "Oh, so many things you read about in books, and *there they are!*"

But Terwilliger was too curious, too avid, just to look. She wanted to know. She spent all the time she could on that trip, including a week in the back country, learning from ranger-naturalists about the landscape and its inhabitants. It would be a lifelong pattern.

Later, married and living in Marin County, Terwilliger made a first step into activism on behalf of her own children. "I realized we needed a playground in the part of Sausalito where we were," she says. Wondering how to proceed, she heard from friends: "Well, you can go down to city council, and you can ask for it. And you've got to learn about city government and what makes it run." She did. The city built a playground.

Thus Terwilliger grasped the disarmingly simple secret of the activist: that she who shows up is heard. Ever after, she went to every meeting she could: city council, planning commission, Marin County board of supervisors. She often went without a fixed agenda. "I would sit in the back row, and I would listen. A lot of times I was the only person there in the audience. Because nobody else was there to talk about an issue, they listened to me. It was wonderful," she recalls. "I got things done." Among other successes, she helped push the county to establish a parks department (lacking until then) and to acquire some choice properties.

In 1957, she helped to found the Marin Audubon Society. Together with Caroline Livermore and others, she worked to prevent the filling of tidelands near Tiburon by creating the Richardson Bay Wildlife Sanctuary, which Audubon administers. Their colleague Marty Griffin called Livermore "the Grand Lady" and Terwilliger "the Bird Lady."

Already, however, Terwilliger was developing another role: that of teacher, the beloved "Mrs. T."

Here, too, she started small, working with the Boy Scouts in Mill Valley, the town at the head of Richardson Bay where her family now lived. She wanted to organize water trips, but access was a problem. Mill Valley

Elizabeth Terwilliger near her home in Mill Valley, 1999

had no boat launch and no publicly owned shore. Terwilliger persuaded the city to buy a piece of land and put in a little pier. "We got the dock and the float here," she says. "Then I got people to teach us how to canoe and how to sail and how to row a boat." But of course she didn't stop there. She brought in nature experts, too. "Don't just look at that water! What's in there? Fishes, crabs, whales? Geese? What else is in there? You learn who goes where. Who is up in the sky, who is in the trees, who is out in the water, who is in the marsh. And you learn to respect things.

"So little by little," says Terwilliger, "I began teaching children myself about the great out-of-doors and how to take care of it." She loves working with the young. "Adults say, 'Where are you going now? What for?' With children you just say, 'Follow me,' and they come."

Soon she developed a practice and a persona. Working with kids throughout Marin, she took them on trips into open space, moving at about half a mile an hour, stopping and examining every rock, log, plant, and visible animal, telling all the stories. As teaching aids, she carried a van full of taxidermied birds and mammals.

"V for a vulture," she says, showing how the bird carries its wings, "Straight out for a hawk.

"Never-in-a-hurry for a seagull, always-in-a-hurry for a duck.

"Remember, terns' wings turn in a circle when they fly.

"If you see a snake that has a jaw like yours and its tail has rattles—Look out!"

Not seldom she found her charges afraid of nature, hypersensitive about things that might bite or sting or charge or frighten. "Knowledge dispels fear," she says, "and this is what you teach children about the out-of-doors, and then they are not afraid."

Terwilliger transmitted her knowledge, on an increasing scale, for thirty-five years. Some Marin families have had three generations walk with Mrs. T. Kids by the million have watched short films of some of her walks. In 1975, a group of volunteers formed the Terwilliger Nature Education Center (now WildCare) to expand and perpetuate her teaching methods. WildCare docents in twelve counties now work with sixty-five thousand children each year.

Living now in a retirement home in Mill Valley, Terwilliger can look out over a marsh she knows and helped to save. She frequently walks on a waterside path. Eyes and ears open as ever, she keeps up a running inventory. "That's a gashawk," she says, using her nickname for an airplane. "That's a jogger. Do you hear the duck? You've got to use all your senses where you are going to go. You don't want to miss anything."

And has she missed anything?

"Not much," says Mrs. T.

Maurice and Jan Holloway

Environmentalists with money, it must be admitted, are a little different from environmentalists without. Though wealthy people may serve their cause also with energy and time, they (and all around them) understand the power of their checkbooks. They speak with a certain wariness, downplaying their own generosity. Moving in high circles of the movement, typically though not always removed from the hurly-burly of specific issues, they also have a little distance from it all—a distance that brings a sometimes enviable clarity.

For Maurice Holloway, whose family firm made the snack food CornNuts, the road to the environment started in the 1940s on northern California lakeshores and stream banks. "As a kid," he remembers, "the excitement was, Gee, where is the next fish going to come from and how big is it going to be? But at the same time I enjoyed just being outside in a place that was pretty much the way it had always been. There was a sense of appropriateness, I think, and peace and quiet."

In the 1950s he began to see how endangered that peace and quiet were. His concern led him to join the Sierra Club and to watch with approval as it grew into a national environmental power.

Though he follows many issues now, Holloway retains a soft spot for rivers. Among his beneficiaries are California Trout, the organization that seeks to protect both wild streams and wild fish; the McCloud River Preserve near Mount Shasta, a Nature Conservancy

area on an unspoiled branch of the Sacramento; and the Smith River on the Oregon border, the only river system in California that is free of dams from headwaters to mouth.

In 1982 Holloway helped the Tuolumne River Preservation Trust make a splash on behalf of a great and threatened river. Downstream from Yosemite National Park, between dams above and below, the Tuolumne flows wild for fifty miles. To raise consciousness and money for the fight against yet another dam, Holloway organized a sweepstakes—first prize: a raft trip—and advertised it on millions upon millions of packages of CornNuts. Since the corn involved came from Central Valley growers inclined to favor the dam, this unconventional move had repercussions. "But people kind of took note of what we were doing and what the Tuolumne River was all about." Holloway thinks the publicity may have helped Congress make the decision to protect the river in 1983.

Holloway has also served as president of The Sierra Club Foundation and has chaired its National Advisory Council. Mostly, though, he has provided financial support and worked behind the scenes.

Jan Holloway—the two were high school sweethearts in San Leandro and married there in 1953—has a slightly different slant on things. The environment that interests her most keenly is the urban one, and at times she has worked as "a kind of foot soldier" in the

123

San Francisco planning wars. In the 1980s she was a leader in the effort to limit high-rise development downtown. She has pounded pavements getting signatures, attended dreary hours of inconclusive meetings, stuffed envelopes. She has profound respect for people who do these things all their lives. "Some people eat that up for breakfast, that kind of fight," she says. But others burn out, and she ruefully counts herself among them. "I really had had it, so again I got a job at an art gallery and then I opened my own. So aside from gnashing my teeth I don't talk much now."

Between them, the Holloways bridge a sometimes troubling gap. Jan says, "There are people outside of the city who feel that the wilder areas are more important. That the city is a city and it's too bad, but we've got more important things to do. And there are people who live their whole lives in the city, and they just want to keep this a place that is affordable and that has parks and that has good transportation and has good air, all

of those things. But there are people"—like herself—"who cross back and forth."

Maurice interrupts. "Let me ask you a question. Why were you down there picketing and opposing high-rise development here in the city? What was there about that that made you so active?"

"San Francisco was so beautiful," Jan replies, "but the buildings were coming—higher and higher." Most activists start like that, she observes, defending something known to them, next door. "But some people take it further. A few people who rise so far above it. Like Amy Meyer, Dorothy Erskine. There are real leaders beyond your own backyard."

The Holloways often speculate about what makes such leaders tick. "I don't know what that quotient is," says Jan. "I think it's a passion they have, that selfless passion. A larger sense of what is important. And they have a feeling of empowerment, that they can affect destiny. I think they are born with it."

Maurice and Jan Holloway at Nicasio Creek in Marin County, 1999

Allan Brown

—ɯ—

As a youngster growing up in Palo Alto in the 1930s, Allan Brown used to climb up a tree in his yard whenever a storm was blowing in. "I would look out and see that the rain was beginning to fall in the west and moving my way. It always rained close to the hills first and then came over our house. I used to think how wonderful it was that we had the winter rains that refreshed everything. I felt lucky to live in such a beautiful place."

As an adult, Brown has done his share to ensure the survival of that beautiful place, and the beautiful world of which it is a part.

His early memories include fishing up and down a stretch of the North Fork of the Kings River (now vanished under a reservoir) and taking part in a Sierra Club work group installing a water line to Parsons Lodge in Tuolumne Meadows. As an adult he went on numerous Club outings, but for many years, he says, he only paid attention to the first two of the three imperatives that make up the organization's motto: *Explore, Enjoy, and Protect.* "I didn't set an example as a grassroots activist like Lennie Roberts or Olive Mayer." But his turn was coming.

It was his friend Mel Lane, retiring from the board of The Sierra Club Foundation, who suggested Brown as a replacement. And so in 1984 he found himself rubbing shoulders with people who had spent lifetimes in the conservation trenches. "If a grassroots activist decides he wants to be a top leader in the Sierra Club, he has to work like mad at the chapter level and do many hard tasks," says Brown. "Gradually, if he is lucky and gets noticed, he can become a chapter chair. Then if he is outstanding as a chapter chair, somebody might ask him if he wants to run for the Sierra Club board. I don't think I'd ever have made it to the top levels of leadership if I'd gone that route! But here I was asked if I wanted to be a trustee."

There were reasons for Brown's ascension, of course: his personal generosity, his business acumen as a Bay Area builder, and his experience in fund-raising. At the time he joined the foundation board, the Sierra Club was nearing the centenary of its 1892 founding, and it seemed an occasion to pass the hat in a big way. None of the usual suspects having stepped forward, Brown became chairman of an arduous but highly successful centennial campaign.

Brown also works on a level closer to his roots. As a member of the board of the Peninsula Open Space Trust, he has helped to preserve many a local forest and farm. He speaks with a kind of paternal affection of

Allan Brown in his backyard in Portola Valley, 1998

127

lands acquired. A recent coup is the acquisition of the Rancho Corral de Tierra on Montara Mountain, at the northern gateway to the San Mateo coastside. The parcel is slated to become part of the Golden Gate National Recreation Area. Then there's the huge Cloverdale Ranch south of Pescadero, which the trust will maintain as open space but lease for environmentally sensitive agriculture. Here purchase was only the start of a story that includes erosion treatments, controlled burns, and elimination of pampas grass, an aggressive and undesired exotic species.

The Peninsula Open Space Trust and its government counterpart, the Midpeninsula Regional Open Space District, are trying to link protected lands along the Santa Cruz Mountains from Montara Mountain to the Santa Cruz County line and beyond, and from the bayside foothills to the sea. The map shows rapid progress toward this goal. Freckles and spatters of green are coalescing into a solid band. Brown would like to see something similar happening on a national scale. He is a supporter of the Wildlands Project, a bold dream to link existing parks, preserves, and ranchlands into continent-spanning green corridors. Nothing less, biologists now say, can truly protect ecosystems in the long run. Brown imagines civilization remade "so that we are living in harmony with nature as opposed to being an impediment and destroyer of all other animals."

But population growth, he fears, could put such dreams out of reach. "We need to work on population worldwide. But there are certain trouble spots where the population is soaring beyond what the world population is doing, and that is happening right here in this country. Of all the developed countries we, by far, have the highest population growth." Brown is one Sierra Club activist who would like it to take stronger stands on population, including a dimmer view of immigration, an issue on which the membership has voted to stay neutral.

For the long term, Brown considers himself an optimist. "Right now we've got a lot of problems. But, yes, I think we will muddle through."

Richard Goldman

—w—

When the philanthropist Richard Goldman is talking about himself, you have to lean forward to hear him. He speaks distinctly but gently, sometimes letting a sentence trail off into silence. But when the subject turns to a cause he believes in, he becomes very audible indeed.

One of the things he believes in most is something he himself exemplifies: cooperation between the corporate and the environmental worlds. "They are going to end up being partners," he says, "and should be, and should always have been. It's just a matter of better understanding and realizing that both have a role to play."

Born and raised in San Francisco, Goldman has spent his life in the insurance business. His late wife, Rhoda, was a descendant of Levi Strauss and a part owner of the family's clothing firm. "We ran into an impasse with Levi Strauss," Goldman says. "They made a change of structure with which we didn't agree. It was opportune to cash out. And we happened to do it when the company seemed to be financially comfortable. Immediately after, it started to slip." The proceeds received, invested elsewhere, multiplied. "We looked upon the money received as a windfall and treated it as such." Part of that windfall, the Goldmans knew, would be invested in the protection of nature.

Like so many people profiled in this book, Richard Goldman received a decisive imprint from an early visit to Yosemite National Park. In 1929, at the age of nine, he was taken on a pack trip to the Ten Lakes Basin in the high country, and he recalls to this day that first of many wilderness excursions. "It wasn't a long hike, but it was just the experience of camping out for a few days. I can't remember much detail. I just remember I enjoyed it immensely." His wife had had similar exposure, and love of the mountains was one of the things that brought the two together when they renewed a childhood acquaintance after World War II.

In later years the couple went back to the Yosemite high country many times, usually out of Tuolumne Meadows, often with children in tow. Before her death in 1996, Rhoda and Richard rafted great rivers, ascended peaks, and even visited Antarctica together near the end.

Much of the environmental work of the Richard and Rhoda Goldman Fund is kept deliberately behind the scenes. The Fund helped acquire the Cargill salt ponds for addition to the San Francisco Bay National Wildlife Refuge. It jump-started the reconstruction of the storm-damaged Conservatory of Flowers in Golden Gate Park. It created a program in Alaska to acquire strategic inholdings in that state's splendid but incompletely protected parks. Few people are aware of the source of the funds that have made these things possible.

But one initiative has made a very public mark on the world: the Goldman Environmental Prize.

"One morning in 1988," Goldman says, "I was reading in the paper about some Nobel awards. And I thought: Is there anything similar to honor people in the environment? I passed it along to the director of our foundation and said, 'See what's out there.' Well, amazingly, there was nothing.

"I've always been impressed that certain prizes have such a tremendous impact, like the Davis Cup in tennis or the Pulitzer Prize in journalism. So we said, 'Let's figure it out.' And we did, and we started it." The first round of awards was given in 1990.

Like the Nobels, and unlike other honors available to environmentalists, the Goldman Awards are given on the planetary scale. There are six, one each for activists from Africa, Asia, Europe, North America, South and Central America, and a grouping called Islands and Island Nations. Goldman calls the winners environmental heroes, and there is nothing empty about that term. While environmentalists in the United States earn our gratitude by giving time or money to the cause, some of the Goldman recipients have sacrificed their freedom and even their lives. The Russian Aleksandr Nikitin and the Mexican Rodolfo Montiel Flores, to name two, paid for their activity with years in jail. On occasion the presentation of the prize, delivered to prison gates, has shamed governments into releasing these political captives. The honor was not enough, however, to save Ken Saro-Wiwa of Nigeria, a literary figure and protestor against the depredations of a ruthless oil industry, from death in 1995 at the hands of a government hangman.

Despite such tragic setbacks, Goldman is optimistic about the future. "I see in the youth of today a tremendous interest in the environment, which is growing every day. They will come into play, and they'll get it done."

At the family home in Atherton grow two tall redwood trees. "One time we took our children on a trip up the Redwood Highway," Goldman recalls, "and we brought back a couple of small trees about the height of that table. It's been wonderful for me to watch them growing every year."

It's tempting to see those trees as symbols of the many things Richard and Rhoda Goldman have helped to grow.

Richard Goldman at home in San Francisco, 1997

Bill and Jean Lane

———ɯ———

Laurence W. Lane always joked that he wanted to be a farmer, not an editor, but had to run a magazine to support his agricultural habit. That magazine was called *Sunset: The Magazine of Western Living*.

Sunset was founded in 1898 by the Southern Pacific Railroad to lure people into the wide-open West. In 1928, ownership passed to Lane, who heeded the message and moved magazine and family from Iowa to the San Francisco Bay Area—where he had his home in Palo Alto and his hobby farm in the Santa Cruz Mountains up behind.

In 1929, the Lanes took their first vacation as Californians. "We went up to Sacramento on the *Delta Queen*," Laurence's son Bill Lane recalls, "and drove up to the Tahoe Tavern at Lake Tahoe. Then over into the Owens Valley and up over Tioga Pass and into Yosemite." To people accustomed to the gentler beauties of the Midwest, "that was quite a revelation." A lifelong family attachment to the Sierra began. In high school in the 1930s, Bill worked for the Forest Service in Mineral King, packing fish on mule back for planting in remote mountain lakes, under the direction of senior packer and future conservation icon Ike Livermore.

Under the Lane family, *Sunset* became the first successful "lifestyle" magazine—a monthly compendium of information and advice about gardens, about cooking, about travel, about parks, about all the gracious components of a leisurely life in the West.

As they matured, Bill and his brother Mel became more and more involved in the magazine. In 1950, young Bill was sent back east to open a *Sunset* office in New York. It was there, on the beach at Fire Island, that he read in the *New Yorker* a series of articles by Rachel Carson that would become her book *The Sea Around Us*. Less famous than her later *Silent Spring*, *The Sea Around Us* was almost equally seminal in its warnings about the effects of human domination of the earth. It made a deep impression on Lane.

In the middle 1950s, the brothers took over day-to-day management of the *Sunset* enterprise. Bill was the magazine's publisher and editor; Mel served as business manager and also brought out the very successful series of Sunset Books.

In 1957, Bill married Donna Jean Gimbel, and they moved to a new hilltop home in Portola Valley, where Bill served a term as mayor. Homeowners in this outlying area faced some typical problems of the urban fringe: deer, fire danger, erosion, figuring out what to grow in hillside gardens. "There were a lot of things we all needed to learn," says Jean. She helped to found the

Bill and Jean Lane at home in Portola Valley, 1998

Westridge Garden Club, which was ahead of its time in promoting the use of native and drought-tolerant plants.

As time went on, *Sunset*'s coverage gained an increasing environmental dimension. The tendency started with the travel stories. It is, after all, a short step from promoting the beauty of a landscape to remarking on threats to that beauty. Thus on one occasion in the 1960s *Sunset* wrote up the Napa Valley wine country but took the occasion to poll its readers: "How would you feel about legislation that would protect those areas from taxes and from future development?" The warm response helped persuade the California legislature to pass the Williamson Act, an early farmland protection measure that lowered taxes for landowners who agreed to defer development. "The Napa Valley would be virtually solid housing now," says Bill Lane, "if that act hadn't been passed, to give those vintners a preferential tax for agricultural land."

Bolder, and more expensive, was the stand *Sunset* took on the chlorinated hydrocarbon pesticides, DDT and its cousins. By 1968 the environmental cost of these powerful, persistent chemicals was becoming clear. "So we ran an article titled 'Blowing the Whistle on DDT,'" Lane recalls. "We took that editorial position. But the toughest decision was to tell Ortho and many of the other pesticide companies that were making pesticides that had these hydrocarbons in them that we would no longer accept their advertising." Coming from the largest single publisher of such ads, this was indeed a shot heard round the world. Senator Gaylord Nelson read *Sunset*'s letter to its advertisers into the *Congressional Record*. It is hard to imagine a major publication taking such a step today.

Soon both brothers were becoming environmental leaders outside the turf of *Sunset* itself. Mel Lane became the first chairman of the San Francisco Bay Conservation and Development Commission and then of the California Coastal Zone Conservation Commission. Bill became a presence on the national scene. As a green Republican, he was called on by presidents of both parties to serve on, and more often than not to chair, a succession of important federal commissions. For instance, he led planning for the 1972 celebration of the centennial of Yellowstone, the first national park. President Ford appointed him the first chairman of a commission to conserve the California desert. The list goes on and on. "I've always been concerned with local environmental issues," says Bill. "I've stayed very close to the state levels of all of our thirteen western states."

These are roles that require a diplomat's skills, and Lane in fact spent four years on the other side of the world, as President Reagan's ambassador to Australia. Speaking of this assignment, this reserved man allows himself a flash of pride: "I think I could say I was a damn good ambassador for Uncle Sam!"

Jean Lane's roles grew in parallel with her husband's. The résumé is long, but she has a special attachment to the Jasper Ridge Biological Preserve on the lands of Stanford University. "It's a 1,200-acre island of biodiversity right here in the middle of the Peninsula, surrounded by suburbia," says Jean. Following the footsteps of her mentor, naturalist Herb Dengler, she has been leading groups there as a docent since 1976.

"One of the most wonderful things I ever purchased," says Jean Lane, "was a hand lens. I never go anywhere without it. The one I have is 30X, so you can look at the inside of a flower and you can see everything, even the tiny mites and little insects that are pollinating, and every part of the flower. I just love to be able to see what's inside everything. So that little instrument has been very useful to me. It has reminded me that there is so much more than what one ordinarily sees within every person and every living thing."

Alfred Heller

In 1947, eighteen-year-old Alfred Heller sat next to a campfire on a Sierra Club High Trip in the Evolution Basin and heard David Brower preach what would later be called environmentalism. After that, Heller knew what side he was on. But in the 1950s, as growth in California exploded, it troubled him that conservationists seemed never to come down from the mountains: that they had so little to say about the shape and problems of the sprawling new metropolitan zones then forming all across America.

What Heller missed in the movement he found in the circle of his parents, public-spirited members of a wealthy San Francisco family. From Catherine Bauer Wurster, a former New Deal housing expert and lecturer at the University of California at Berkeley, he absorbed the gospel of planning: that some basic decisions about how and where we live just have to be made centrally to be made at all well. Call it "the people" or call it "the government"—the community, and not the would-be developers, must be in charge. "Planning, as a rational way of coordinating different needs and different interests, had an appeal to me," he says.

In 1957, after a few years back east, Heller and his wife, Ruth, moved to Nevada City in the northern Sierra foothills to found a newspaper. He soon found himself in the middle of a freeway battle.

This was the heyday of freeway expansion, and the state of California planned a highway network linking every county seat. This quaintly Cartesian vision—unrelated to where the traffic actually was—demanded a big road through little Nevada City. Heller and his *Nevada County Nugget* fought the project. He lost—so he says—but the highway that was finally built was considerably less brutal than the design initially proposed.

The controversy taught Heller how much harm could be done by good intentions pursued with blinders on. "As we did the fight, it was very easy to see that state transportation policy had no connection with any other state policy, whether it was natural resource policy or urban development policy or social policies of one kind or another." If the pieces were not brought together, Heller saw, the results were all too likely to be bad. "That's when I started talking about starting an organization that would discuss the need for coordinated state policies for development that took the environment into account." The person he mostly talked with was Sam Wood, an eloquent planning advocate in the Wurster circle and a consultant to the Republican majority in the legislature.

In 1961, Heller and Wood started an organization called California Tomorrow, with Heller's initial financial support. It set up offices in Sacramento and started making its case.

Its very first statement was probably its most influential: an exposé of the effects of unmanaged growth titled *California, Going, Going . . .* Wurster brought it to the attention of *San Francisco Chronicle* editor Scott Newhall, who ran big chunks of it verbatim. Excerpts appeared in newspapers statewide.

"It really kind of grabbed people's attention," says Heller. "We coined the word *slurbs*, which we defined as 'sloppy, sleazy, slovenly, slipshod semi-cities,' and that created a lot of interest. And we brought in things about, Hey, this freeway system stinks! and Look at these subdivisions running wild over farmlands! People hadn't heard that stuff yet. It's hard to imagine, now."

A stream of other such publications followed, and for a decade California Tomorrow was an influential voice on the California scene. But it proved much easier to excite alarm about what was happening to the state than it was to sell Heller's and Wood's centralized planning remedies. Most discouraging of all was the reaction within the planning guild. "So many people, planners that we knew who should have known better, were always saying, 'I don't know how you do a state plan, you can't do a state plan, it's impossible.'"

Heller decided that California Tomorrow, on its own, should demonstrate how such a plan might be created and what it might contain. The result, called *The California Tomorrow Plan*, appeared in 1971. Along with numerous specific policies, it sketched, in remarkable detail, a revised system of government for California. The state would set the basic outlines of land use by zoning most land for one of three purposes, "urban," "agricultural," and "conservation." Ten new regional governments, with elected legislatures, would manage development within this framework and make many of the decisions now entrusted to 534 city and county governments and several thousand special districts and agencies up and down the state.

The *California Tomorrow Plan* was received rapturously by some and respectfully by many. It appeared at a moment when reform was already in the air. Special government bodies were established about this time to protect San Francisco Bay from fill and the entire California coast from urban sprawl. Bills for a limited regional government for the San Francisco Bay Area, the most receptive region, were seriously debated in the legislature. A strong farmland protection law came close to enactment. But in the end a modest tinkering was all that could be achieved.

"You're going against every local governmental interest in pushing for regional government," Heller acknowledges. "And it was the height of the Cold War. Anybody who wanted state planning, and a regional authority, and a new layer of government—it all sounded a little like the Russian Five-Year Plan or whatever."

Thirty years later, the state population has doubled, and the wave of haphazard development California Tomorrow warned about has moved east into the agricultural heartland. Most decisions about growth are made, as before, in a decentralized free-for-all. But there is a little renewed traffic on the trails blazed by Alfred Heller and Sam Wood. There is a growing sense in Sacramento that the system is broken. The Sierra Club has identified urban sprawl as a national issue. ("Welcome to the *twentieth* century," Heller says acerbically.) The "Green Planning" advocated by Huey Johnson and the Resource Renewal Institute has considerable overlaps with the old California Tomorrow thinking.

The challenge issued by California Tomorrow when it published its great document in 1971 remains valid: "Are you making a better plan?"

Alfred Heller at Lagunitas Lake in Marin County, 1998

136

Huey Johnson

—⁓—

Huey Johnson's friend on the board of The Nature Conservancy, the renowned land-saving organization, was not pleased. "Dear Huey," the note began. "You have probably just bankrupted the Conservancy. You have put us out of business. And if it wasn't for the fact that we have to raise a million dollars, we would fire you!"

The year was 1967. What Huey Johnson had done was to commit the organization, at the time still small and unsteady on its feet, to a breathtaking purchase: the acquisition of a pristine 8,000-acre rainforest canyon called Kipahulu Valley on the island of Maui. As the sole conservancy staffer west of the Mississippi, Johnson had found himself confronted with a scary opportunity and had seized it with both hands.

Johnson threw himself into the campaign. He sent ornithologists into the untracked jungle in search of photogenic birds previously thought extinct; the birds were found and publicized. He recruited celebrities, including the aged Charles Lindbergh, a Hawaii enthusiast who now is buried near the valley. He pitched the cause to America's richest families and at a single memorable luncheon raised half the needed sum. Today, Kipahulu Valley is an icon and part of Haleakala National Park.

That victory put The Nature Conservancy on the national environmental map. Instead of losing his job, Johnson was offered the organization's presidency—and turned it down because it would mean moving from San Francisco to Washington D.C.

Johnson grew up in Michigan during the years of Depression and war. He learned the love of nature from his mother. "I can remember her showing me a forest that was growing that she had been part of, planting it, as a child in school. Now the trees were this big. And she used to take me there to play," he says.

Like most kids of the era, Johnson also learned early the habit of hard work. He hoed sugar beets, sold brushes, hauled garbage, painted bridges. He vowed, though, to find a task in life that he could pursue with passion. On the way to that vocation, he brilliantly began and abruptly dropped a sales career at Union Carbide, spent two years traveling around the world, resolved to become a teacher, and pursued a doctorate at the University of Michigan. It was there that he spotted a Nature Conservancy flyer seeking candidates for a post in San Francisco, a city he had visited and loved. "I walked into the nearest phone booth and within a few days had the job. I left academia and headed west, never to look back or be sorry."

Huey Johnson outside the Golden Gate, 1997

139

In his years with the Conservancy, Johnson oversaw the preservation of key pieces of land in his adopted home region, notably around the Golden Gate. It was the Conservancy that picked up the pieces when the massive Marincello development in the Marin Headlands fell through. "I got the option to buy this $12 million, 2,000-acre parcel," Johnson marvels, "with a $100 personal check."

As The Nature Conservancy grew bigger and, he felt, more staid, Johnson began to itch for the risk-taking style with which he had begun. In 1972, he founded a new group, the Trust for Public Land. TPL pioneered a novel kind of land acquisition, taking on the complex, messy cases: small parcels, urban lands, divided ownerships, multiple uses. In short order he built this organization, too, into a major power.

But Johnson's itch to action was unstilled. He felt the need to influence the world now on a larger scale, through government policy. "I had spent a lot of time fighting against one bulldozer or another. If I got a policy regulation in place, I could affect ten thousand bulldozers and what a bulldozer could legally do."

The door he was looking for opened in 1974, when governor-elect Jerry Brown asked Johnson to be his secretary of resources, succeeding Reagan's able Ike Livermore. It is hard to think of two public servants more different in style.

"I said, 'Jerry, I'm not going to stand in line to get your permission to do anything. If you don't like what I'm doing, fire me.' If I wanted to talk to him, I'd issue a press release. Everyone in the cabinet had a red phone on their desk, and he would call on that and say, 'What are you doing?'"

Johnson recalls some successes from that time, notably getting a thousand miles of rivers placed off limits to dams in the state and federal Wild Rivers systems, and some failures, like an unsuccessful effort to tighten protection of wetlands. "I had a great time in government. And was glad to leave it."

Along the way, Johnson had come to a breathtaking conclusion: "I realized at some point that humanity had accumulated enough wisdom and new tools to solve the environmental problem—to put it behind us." The environmental problem. Note the singular. Johnson sees all the familiar roster of ills as aspects of a single disorder, which can only be addressed comprehensively, by attacking all its elements at once. "If we only do one open space, one of these things at a time, the whole place falls apart," he says.

"I wandered the world looking for better ways of doing things. Really found it in the Netherlands, where they have a plan for total environmental recovery in twenty-five years. They put their best minds to work: engineers, scientists, financiers, to come up with a plan at every level: soil, air, water, fisheries, transportation. They are fifteen years into a twenty-five year plan and it's remarkably on target."

To help define and share this wisdom, these tools, Johnson founded his last large organization, the Resource Renewal Institute, headquartered at Fort Mason in San Francisco. Its mission might be defined as teaching the world to think like the Dutch. The "Green Planning" idea has entered into official thinking in several countries around the world, but not yet, despite the efforts of the institute, on any large scale in the United States.

Another of Johnson's organizations is the Aldo Leopold Society, named for the famous naturalist who was also, less famously, an avid fisherman and hunter. Johnson likewise unites these interests. "I decided at some point that somebody was killing my meat," he says, "and maybe I should be the one doing it." The Leopold Society embodies "an enlightened view of hunting, fishing, and gathering."

Doris Leonard

—⁂—

Doris Leonard's conversation circles back and back to a moment on the North Slope of Alaska in 1969. Oil had been discovered in the region the previous year, and the rush was on to build a trans-Alaska pipeline to bring it south. Leonard had come north to see the landscape these events would alter. "Sitting up there as I did at the very top of the world, by myself, looking out over a sea of ice, nothing but ice, I had this feeling that I was the only person in the world. I was just sitting there, and I was going to be taken care of."

Doris Leonard came to that shiversome spot by way of a San Francisco childhood and a fortunate marriage. Already as a young girl she was subliminally learning the outdoors. Her family lived near Golden Gate Park and traveled seven weeks each summer, camping in the western states—once, in 1922, in Alaska—when camping was just a matter of pulling off the road. "My mother was the one who impressed me with what I was seeing," says Leonard. "She was a fine gardener, and so she knew the names of the wildflowers and passed it along."

In 1932, at a government agency where both worked briefly, she met the outdoorsman and conservationist Dick Leonard. He almost immediately taught her to rock climb. Indeed, you might say, he taught everybody west of the Rockies to rock climb. With companions Jules Eichhorn and David Brower, Leonard founded the Cragmont Climbing Club and

introduced to the region the safety techniques that still are used today.

Doris and Dick were married in 1934 and spent their honeymoon climbing in the North Cascades. "There is a picture of the two of us on top of Cleaver Peak," Leonard recalls. "It was one of these cameras that you set, and then you run up to get into it. He had to climb quite a steep bit to get up to where I was sitting. And I heard the doggone thing click, and I said, 'Well that got a nice picture of your rump!' But it was a beautiful picture. He had turned around and turned on his lovely smile."

Dick became more and more deeply involved in Sierra Club conservation affairs, and Doris, busy with family, was content to be a sidekick for a while. By the 1950s, however, she was developing distinct roles. She chaired a succession of conferences on wilderness protection, meetings that would help produce that great charter, the Wilderness Act of 1964. She organized the first World Conference on National Parks. And in 1962, with partners George Collins and Dorothy Varian, she set up a pioneer nonprofit land-buying organization, Conservation Associates.

At that time, The Nature Conservancy was a struggling eastern organization, and such outfits as the Trust for Public Land weren't even thought of. The Save the Redwoods League (in which both Leonards were active) was specialized. Lacking was a nimble,

general-purpose body that could buy key lands, sometimes from under the noses of developers, and hold them until park agencies had the funds to take over title. Conservation Associates set out to fill the void. Its proudest moment may have been the acquisition of several key parcels at Point Reyes National Seashore at a moment when the new park seemed at risk of becoming an empty shell.

Leonard, who was also a founding member of the Point Reyes National Seashore Association, retains a special fondness for Point Reyes. "I had that park almost to myself when we were working on it, to raise the money to buy the first pieces of land." She pauses. "I didn't think Point Reyes was going to be the success that it is. Because there are no roadways in there; you have to hike a lot. I thought, people today don't do that. They need to have an automobile." She is glad to have been proved wrong.

Conservation Associates made its mark to the south of San Francisco, too. "Big Basin—we added acres and acres to Big Basin State Park. Castle Rock State Park—we started that, and we carried it through to its inclusion in the State Parks System." The Forest of Nisene Marks State Park, a 10,000-acre reserve along Aptos Creek, exists because a family approached the Associates to create a memorial to their mother.

Doris Leonard recalls driving home with her grandchildren from a mountain trip in the Sierra. "I said, 'Look over there, Sam. See that lovely oak hill?' He said, 'Yeah, Grandma.' I said, 'Well, look at it, because when you are my age it won't be there.' He sort of jumped back; he hadn't thought of that. So I said, 'Unless somebody like my office buys it.'"

Then, Alaska. As for Ed and Peggy Wayburn, the "Great Land" was a revelation to the Leonards. By 1970, the great piñata of the northern wilderness was about to be cracked open. Doris was one of the many who rallied to limit the environmental cost and to save some of the grandest shards as parks and wildlife refuges. Her particular concern was the Central Arctic herd of caribou that swept twice yearly along the Alaskan north slope on their annual migrations. The oil pipeline would bisect its range. Would it split and decimate the population as the transcontinental railroad once split and decimated the bison? Would the animals, trapped and frustrated by the pipeline, become unduly easy prey for their natural predators, the wolves?

She had an idea that animal underpasses every few miles would help. The thought ran into skepticism from the oil companies (who feared the expense), from biologists (who doubted the effectiveness), and from engineers (who pointed out the difficulties of tunneling in permafrost). But her friend A. Starker Leopold at U.C. Berkeley, an authority on ungulates, backed her up. Conservationists insisted, and the tunnel-equipped pipeline has had less effect on the herd than many feared.

"Are you proud of what you have done?" Doris Leonard is asked.

"I am. I am proud."

Doris Leonard at home in Berkeley, 1998

Put Livermore

When Putnam Livermore was serving in the Pacific Theater of World War II, he got letters from his mother, Caroline, the eminent Marin County conservationist, describing her own battles—for parks, open space, and planning. She drew a parallel: both were fighting, in their different ways, for their country and what was best about it.

Parks as patriotism. It's a theme that has fallen out of use—but one that could stand some reviving.

Back home after the war, Put Livermore finished his law studies and went to work for the San Francisco firm of Chickering & Gregory, where fifty years later he is senior partner. One day he had lunch with Dick and Doris Leonard, whom he had gotten to know before the war around Sierra Club campfires ("as Ike Livermore's little brother," Put recalls). The Leonards were starting up Conservation Associates, a new nonprofit organization to preserve endangered landscapes. Looking for a lawyer to help with this work, they said, "Let's get Put." Livermore was thrilled. "That was one of the great moments of my life," he says.

The way it worked was this. Doris Leonard and her cohorts would scout California for parcels worthy of preservation that might be available. After preliminary contacts, they'd come to Livermore. "And then we'd have lunch in a restaurant and they'd explain it to me and I'd put it together." Putting it together could involve months of patient work and negotiations, both with the landowners and with the public agencies that, at the end of the process, would take the land and reimburse the Conservation Associates go-betweens.

As The Nature Conservancy became active in California, Livermore began serving the same function for that organization; later, he helped incorporate the Trust for Public Land.

Livermore's work with sometimes eccentric owners gave him a stock of stories. One figure who stands out is Heath Angelo, owner of a 6,000-acre property on the South Fork of the Eel River, now known as the Angelo Preserve. "He was one of these guys who just love the land so much, they're mystical characters," Livermore says. He recalls driving up one weekend to see Angelo and straighten out a snag. "We talked about politics and conservation. We talked Friday night and all day Saturday. And Sunday morning I said, 'Mr. Angelo, how about the deed. We've paid you for the land. I've got to get the deed.' 'Oh my God,' he said, 'I thought you were going to stay a couple of weeks, and we were going to negotiate this thing!'" It was years, in fact, before the last loose end was tied up.

Put Livermore at Sweeney Ridge, above Pacifica, in the Golden Gate National Recreation Area, 2004

Livermore's work with the land conservation organizations brought him many satisfying moments. He counts among his proudest achievements the acquisition of the Forest of Nisene Marks State Park near Aptos, Molera State Park at the mouth of the Big Sur River, and the Wilkins Ranch near Bolinas for the Golden Gate National Recreation Area. The last required uncommonly quick work. Congressman Phillip Burton had announced that a certain sum was available for acquisition of a certain acreage, which threatened in effect to set the per-acre price: an unduly high one, Livermore thought. Working with an appraiser in Reno, he had the land optioned to the Trust for Public Land within a week. By establishing a moderate land value for the rest of the national recreation area, the deal saved the public millions of dollars.

Then there were the salt ponds. In 1972, Congress had created the San Francisco Bay National Wildlife Refuge—some twenty-three thousand acres—on both shores of southern San Francisco Bay. However, half of the territory in the new refuge was diked-off wetlands, once marsh, now solar evaporation ponds used to produce salt. Many birds used the ponds, and the plan was not to end salt making, but merely to make sure that the land could not be filled and developed. Working with Leslie Salt and with Rodney Hamblin, the Assistant U.S. Attorney in San Francisco, Livermore finally found language that both sides would accept, giving the government the title but leaving the company in control of its salt-making operations.

Livermore regards this transaction, completed in 1979, as his biggest coup.

In the early 1980s, Livermore managed the acquisition of Sweeney Ridge above Pacifica for the Golden Gate National Recreation Area. It was from this hilltop that the Spanish explorer Gaspar de Portolá sighted San Francisco Bay in 1769. Though the land was a vital greenbelt link, the government blew hot and cold about buying it, and the owner wasn't all that keen on selling it. Livermore credits Harriet Burgess of Trust for Public Land with the sheer doggedness that kept the conversation going for several years until he could finally close the deal in 1985.

Along the way, he became an expert in the matter of conservation easements, restrictions placed on land by an owner, as a condition of sale, or by a buyer, who purchases limited rights to achieve a goal. At Nisene Marks, the family agreed to sell the land at far below market value—if its ideas about management were written into the deed. In the more common case, a conservation buyer pays an owner to give up development rights, preserving open space while leaving land in private hands. In 1983, Livermore coauthored a landmark book on this subject, *The Conservation Easement in California*, published by the Trust for Public Land.

The art of land preservation has indeed matured since the days of Conservation Associates, and Put Livermore has had a lot to do with its refinement, in theory and in practice.

Martin Litton

Lives in conservation are often lives of physical adventure. Not always, certainly, but often enough to make you wonder if there is some hormonal link. Martin Litton, who somehow survived to become an elder statesman of the movement, is a case in point.

Growing up in the countryside near Los Angeles after World War I, Litton suffered frostbite on the windy ridges of the San Gabriel Mountains and survived an 80-foot plunge over a waterfall. Though colorblind, he cheated his way through examinations to become a glider pilot in World War II. In the 1950s, he began rowing the rapids of the Grand Canyon, first on his own, then as a guide and outfitter. In 1965, he added his name to the short list of those who had gone through the famous Lava Falls in a small wooden boat.

Litton's conservation interests grew in tandem with his outdoor exploits. As a high school student he already worried, he says, "about all the web of roads on the map. There wasn't any space in between them. So by the time I got to UCLA, a classmate named Norm Padgett and I created an organization called California Trails. We started it because they were building this Angeles Crest Highway through the San Gabriel Mountains, and it was going to wipe out wilderness." Their protest failed to stop the highway, but the club stayed in existence, and later helped block several roads in the Sierra Nevada.

In college, young Litton heard from a fellow member of the rowing team, the son of a city engineer, about Los Angeles's plans for Mono Lake. The city was about to divert the streams feeding this fascinating inland sea, which lies three hundred miles north along the eastern slope of the Sierra, to add to urban water supply. Litton fired off a prescient letter of protest to the *Los Angeles Times*. "Here was this eighteen-year-old kid," he marvels, "telling officialdom what it's got to do about Mono Lake—which nobody had ever heard of at that time!"

After the war, Litton always made at least part of his living with camera and typewriter. In 1954, he went to work for *Sunset* magazine and helped to give that publication its subtle pro-conservation tilt.

In the 1960s, he was absorbed in the battle to create a Redwood National Park on Redwood Creek north of Eureka, where grow the tallest trees now standing in the world. That fact came out during the debate, almost by accident.

In those days conservationists were split about the best site for a Redwood National Park. The Save-the-Redwoods League proposed to base the federal preserve on existing state parks near Crescent City. The Sierra Club faction, including Litton and Ed Wayburn, wanted to save more trees and more acreage on Redwood Creek. Some local logging companies, meanwhile, were trying to make both plans unworkable by

building roads and cutting trees in every corner of the region. The strategy almost succeeded.

Litton remembers the day he stood on the banks of Redwood Creek with a top Park Service official, looking at a depressing vista of stumps. "There wasn't anything virgin for any distance in the redwoods by then," he says. "You had to get little bits and pieces and then hope it would grow up in between and look something like the way nature created it.

"So he was saying, 'Martin, I don't know; right across the creek here it's all logged off; it looks awful.' I said, 'Well, it doesn't look awful *here*. And for all you know, this could be the tallest tree in the world.' And I slapped the tree we happened to be standing beside. I had no idea how tall it was, you know. And being a bureaucrat, the way their minds work! He took a team of surveyors back in there and measured it, and it was the tallest tree that had ever been measured up to that time." That led to a cover story, invaluable to the cause, in *National Geographic*. Park backers were pleased to let the National Geographic Society take credit for the discovery.

Partly because conservationists were so divided, the national park created in 1968 included only the bottomlands of Redwood Creek, a narrow, winding, vulnerable strip that everyone called "the worm." Eight years later, the surrounding slopes were brought in, pretty much stripped of old redwoods but capable of restoration, which has since made great strides.

Thinking back on those times, Litton muses: "You have hard battles. You not only fight your enemies, but you fight your friends."

The biggest fight among friends in the 1960s was the split within the Sierra Club as to whether to oppose the Diablo Canyon nuclear power plant on a rugged shore near San Luis Obispo. Eminent Club leaders—Edgar Wayburn, Richard Leonard, Will Siri, Ansel Adams—wanted no part of this fight. Equally eminent conservationists, including Litton and David Brower, then the Club's executive director, demanded that the issue be taken on. The matter was decided in 1967 by a membership vote, which went against Brower and his allies. Decades later, Litton is still bitter. "It was the biggest issue in my life." It took years, and the rise of new leaders to whom the battle was just history, to heal the scars within the Sierra Club.

Litton went on to work on many other issues, including the preservation of the giant sequoias of the Sierra Nevada. Among his perennial causes are mining law reform, the acquisition of inholdings in the National Forests, and preservation of the jungles of Surinam.

He worries about the young and the leveling mass culture that seems to engulf them, but declines to advise. "I don't think they can be told. The problem is, if you're not on fire about things, what's going to light it? Not having some old fogy come along and tell you what to do." He's a bit nonplussed to be regarded as a guru by budding environmentalists. "They either are or they pretend to be awfully admiring and wanting to hang on every word.

"But I never did that with anybody. How come they do?"

Martin Litton at the Palo Alto Airport, 1997

David Brower

—ᴍ—

In 1947, David Ross Brower led a Sierra Club backpacking trip to the Evolution Basin region of the central Sierra. Young Alfred Heller was along and remembers the journey well. "Going between camps there would be the designated trail and then the Brower shortcut. Dave would choose cross-country routes over passes, which on the map looked like shortcuts, but of course were nothing like shortcuts. But the views were great, commanding views, and the energy was high."

In the same words you might describe David Brower's life and his conservation career.

Born in 1912, Brower grew up in Berkeley and remembers the Berkeley Hills when they were wild. He remembers family camping trips to the Sierra when Lake Tahoe was four days away. And he remembers the spring he found and lost on the road to Donner Summit, "just coming out of the dirt, good, clear, clean, crystal-clean water. I was impressed. But the next time we went by there they had logged that place and the spring was gone. And that began to worry me, those forests and what was happening to them."

As a teenager, Brower worked at a summer camp near Lake Tahoe and took groups into what is now the Desolation Wilderness. And he began to climb rock, none too safely, as he recalls. In 1933, heeding the urgent advice of a friend, he joined the Sierra Club to get some instruction. He also spent summers in Yosemite Valley in those Depression years, working for the Yosemite Park and Curry Company and hanging out in the studio of photographer and conservationist Ansel Adams, talking of f-stops and wilderness.

During the 1940s, besides fighting with the Tenth Mountain Division in Italy, Brower worked as an editor at University of California Press (where he met his wife, Anne). In his spare time he did increasing amounts of work for the Sierra Club and edited its magazine, then called the *Bulletin*. In 1952, he left U.C. Press to become the Sierra Club's executive director.

By then Brower had developed a sense of terrible urgency. "What we save in the next ten years," he liked to say, "is all that will ever be saved." He said that for several decades running.

During his tenure, and largely through his energy, the Sierra Club evolved from an outings club with a conservation sideline into a national environmental force. Brower managed the battles against dams in Dinosaur National Monument and in the Grand Canyon, launched the influential and elegant "exhibit format" series of books about wilderness, became an icon to the young, and found himself facing growing

David Brower at home in Berkeley, 1997

tensions with his boss, the Sierra Club's elected board of directors.

In his drive to promote the cause, he brushed off the critics who felt he was spending too much, taking center stage too much, and in general getting the Club out on too many limbs. In 1967, he found himself on the losing side in the debate over whether to oppose the Diablo Canyon nuclear power plant on a scenic stretch of coast near San Luis Obispo. By 1969, the Club was in schism, with formal pro- and anti-Brower parties campaigning for control of its elective board. The Brower slate lost, and he was out of a job.

Brower went on to launch several other very effective environmental organizations, including Friends of the Earth and the League of Conservation Voters; yet he is only secondarily (and perhaps never quite comfortably) an organization man. His talent is rather that of a visionary, seeing the big picture, demanding, articulating, refusing to see limits or respect sensibilities, reporting to no board. Even in old age, he is the man to get things going, to make connections, to fire up a crowd.

Wherever Brower goes, he forms a kind of conservation salon. His table talk, like his writing, is full of aphorisms and epiphanies. Certain logical leaps and simplifications can give pause. But you have to hear him almost as a poet, like the Robinson Jeffers he so admired, or a prophet, like Isaiah, "one of the best writers in the Bible," whom he frequently calls to witness.

"One of my two favorite Isaiah quotes," he says, "is about population: 'Thou hast multiplied the nation and not increased the joy.' This is so powerful! The other is about wilderness and sprawl. 'Woe unto them who join house to house and lay field to field, till there be no place where they may be placed alone in the midst of the earth.'

"The most important issue globally is our addiction to the drug of growth. We think everything has to be bigger to be better. I don't quite know when that idea began to fester, but it is one of the worst ones we ever came up with. The population of the earth has gone up by a factor of three in my lifetime. In California, a factor of sixteen. This won't work."

The monotheistic religions, Brower notes, took shape when population was small and the conservation of nature not an issue. They need an update. "When are we going to go back up the mountain," he asks, "and bring down the other tablet—the one that Moses forgot? The Ten Commandments are entirely about how we deal with each other, not a word about how we deal with the planet. So it must be there; we just need to find the right one."

Also in need of an update are conventional economic ideas. "The problem is that our economists have not yet learned what it is going to cost not to do the things we must do. That just escapes them." Economics as we know it, he says, "is a form of mental illness."

Publication of his 1995 book *Let the Mountains Talk, Let the Rivers Run* gave Brower a chance to make a practical stand. After a brisk argument, he persuaded the publisher to print the work on paper made from kenaf, which costs more in dollars but less in environmental terms than paper from trees.

One favorite Brower theme is the need for alliances between conservationists and organized labor. A chance for convergence came in 1999, when both groups found themselves fighting Charles Hurwitz's Maxxam Corporation. One of Maxxam's many corporate arms was logging Northern California redwoods with a rapacity not seen for decades; another was locking steelworkers out of mills. The aggrieved parties got together in the Alliance for Sustainable Jobs and the Environment, with leadership drawn equally from the two worlds. Brower is co-chair. "It is going to take the combined power of labor and the environmental movement, at least, to get a little bit of balance, to overcome the enormous power that has gone to Wall Street. Corporations," he adds, "not only should have the rights of people but they should have the conscience of people."

Always the writer, Brower is a foe to jargon, including the word *environmentalism*. "We lost the conservation movement when we called ourselves environmentalists. Too many syllables. Environmentalist. It's just frightful!" Asked about his "spirituality," he reacts in the same way. "Too many syllables. I like *spirit*, *spiritual*. *Spirituality* is getting to be a business.

"We are a rather talented species," he goes on. "We do have a conscience. We have a soul. Don't quite know where it sits. We have heart, have mind." And where does spirit fit into this? "It should never leave. You shouldn't have to think about it, any more than you have to think about how to swallow."

Brower advises his fellow activists not to be too hard on themselves. "I say count the things you have done, not the things you haven't done. The things you haven't done is an endless list. Everybody needs at least one consecutive success. Feel good about what you are doing."

Young people, he suggests, can help best by importing green values into whatever career they choose. "Do whatever you are going to do. Get going in that profession. In whatever the field, make them aware of what the earth needs." Since the system is rigged against environmental protection, a little counter-rigging is justified. "Cheat!" David Brower says, with a hint of a grin. "Cheat our way!"

Edgar Wayburn

—⁓—

The people in this book have many things, 90 percent of them nice things, to say about one another. But one name more than any other is singled out for praise: Ed Wayburn. Allan Brown: "Ed Wayburn to me is just a wonderful environmentalist, from the core of himself." Frances Spangle: "He is an example of the best, I think, because he is able to pay attention to very small things, but also to operate on a national and international scale." Martin Rosen says simply, "Edgar Wayburn is a hero of mine."

The object of all this affection was born in 1906 in Georgia and came to California to practice medicine in 1933. He was instantly struck by "the marvelous coastal area around San Francisco," and a first visit to Yosemite Valley brought tears to his eyes. He joined the Sierra Club in 1939, initially in order to go on a pack trip. After service in World War II, he returned to find his adopted home region changing fast. "Starting in 1946," says Wayburn, "I was a confirmed environmentalist, or conservationist, as we called them in those days."

His first concern was "the hills of home," especially Mount Tamalpais in Marin County. Part of the landmark mountain was parkland, but most of its lower slopes were in dairy farms. "Don't worry," Wayburn was told. "These people have been here forever and will always keep their ranches." "Three months later I heard about the acquisition of one of the ranches by speculators. That really got me going." Wayburn sat down and drafted an ideal future boundary for the state park, including the entire watershed of its major stream, Redwood Creek. It took a quarter century, but this vision of protection was finally fulfilled.

It was in Tamalpais State Park that Wayburn introduced his future wife, Peggy Elliott, to the pleasures of hiking, and to the conservation cause.

The next Wayburn campaign was centered on a far greater Redwood Creek, the one in Humboldt County on whose banks grow the tallest trees in the world. The need was to protect, not only the great sequoias themselves, but the slopes above them and the streams that flowed down into them. Bitter experience had showed how "protected" groves could be lost to erosion if surrounding watersheds were logged. Though a Redwood National Park was created in 1968, it took another ten years to achieve the minimum viable boundaries.

In 1970, Amy Meyer of San Francisco came to seek Wayburn's help in stopping a utilitarian building planned for East Fort Miley, a parcel of vacant military land near her home. Wayburn recognized this seemingly minor issue as part of a major one: the piecemeal

Edgar Wayburn with his wife, Peggy, on Tracy Arm fjord near Juneau, Alaska, 1998

development that was nibbling away at the scenic Army forts around the Golden Gate. In 1971, Wayburn and Meyer formed People for the Golden Gate National Recreation Area to push for a federal park including the forts and some additional land in Marin County as well. But how much additional land? "We plotted out some alternative park boundaries and offered them to Congressman Phillip Burton," Wayburn recalls. "The first plan I offered him, he looked up at me and said, 'Is this what you want?' I said, 'No.' He said, 'Why don't you tell me what you want?' I said I didn't think it was feasible. He said, 'Don't tell me what's feasible. You tell me what you want and I'll get it through Congress.'" Sixteen months later, a maximal Golden Gate National Recreation Area, stretching all the way to Point Reyes and incorporating the ranches of the Olema Valley, was a reality. "The GGNRA," Wayburn says, "was the happiest of all my campaigns.

"I look back on the 1970s," he goes on, "with a certain amount of awe. I wonder how I practiced medicine while doing those various things." Besides the California issues, he and Peggy were hard at work on the biggest cause of all: a wholesale set-aside of parks and wilderness areas in Alaska.

The Wayburns visited Alaska first in 1967 and "were overwhelmed by the magnificence of the country." Alaska was not only full of grand scenery, mostly unprotected; it was also the one place in the United States where one could still dream of setting aside preserves on an ecosystem scale: whole vast watersheds, the entire ranges of migrating caribou herds, treasuries of wilderness. "There is no national park in the Lower 48 large enough to permanently protect what it has inside," says Wayburn. Alaska could be different.

Rather than working in the traditional way, one area at a time, Wayburn envisioned a grand slam called the Alaska National Interest Lands Conservation Act.

The Sierra Club board of directors, which he headed at the time, made it a top priority. "For thirteen years Alaska was the centerpiece of Sierra Club conservation efforts," Wayburn says. In the fall of 1980, as voters prepared to elect a president, the act had passed in two rival versions: a House plan that contained virtually everything conservationists desired and a more modest version in the Senate. The victory of Ronald Reagan tipped the balance for the weaker bill. Even that, Wayburn notes, was the largest conservation act in American history, setting aside some 104 million acres under one protective designation or another.

Ed Wayburn muses on the way the environmental vision has expanded. In the beginning, he notes, "we just knew there were certain exceptional, special places that had to be protected." The next step was to think in terms of whole watersheds, as at the two Redwood Creeks. Then in terms of ecosystems, as in Alaska. The next generation, he thinks, must focus on the entire world.

"Young people today have an extraordinary opportunity," says Wayburn. "Most of the special places of scenic magnificence have been protected or else they are lost. But we know now that it isn't just the conservation of natural resources, it's the entire environment that is important. The air, the water, the forest, the land. It's all interconnected. Their work has to be on parts or all of that great interconnection which is our earth.

"Population is increasing all too fast, and I have seen no signs of it abating enough to sustain all the people we will have, or even the number we have at the present time, with our pattern of consumption. But at the same time this is an opportunity for people to participate in drafting what must be a new world order.

"We need to work particularly in our own country, but also to help in other countries where needed, without intruding ourselves. Not to go as emissaries from the United States, but as citizens of the world."

INDEX

ABOUT THE PHOTOGRAPHER AND THE AUTHOR

—⁓—

Nancy Kittle studied at the San Francisco Art Institute and has exhibited at the Falkirk Gallery in San Rafael and the Bay Model Visitor Center in Sausalito. She resides in Mill Valley, California.

John Hart is a conservationist, poet, backpacker, and climber, and the author of numerous books, including *Walking Softly in the Wilderness: The Sierra Club Guide to Backpacking* and *San Francisco Bay: Portrait of a Changing Estuary*. He lives in San Rafael, California.